Kwa Heri Means Goodbye

Kwa Heri Means Goodbye

◆

Memories of Kenya 1957-1959

Dorothy Stephens

iUniverse, Inc.
New York Lincoln Shanghai

Kwa Heri Means Goodbye
Memories of Kenya 1957-1959

iUniverse books may be ordered through booksellers or by contacting:

iUniverse
2021 Pine Lake Road, Suite 100
Lincoln, NE 68512
www.iuniverse.com
1-800-Authors (1-800-288-4677)

The views expressed in this work are solely those of the author and do not necessarily reflect the views of the publisher, and the publisher hereby disclaims any responsibility for them.

ISBN-13: 978-0-595-41517-5 (pbk)
ISBN-13: 978-0-595-85866-8 (ebk)
ISBN-10: 0-595-41517-2 (pbk)
ISBN-10: 0-595-85866-X (ebk)

Printed in the United States of America

TO KELLY

Taking our daughter Kelly to Kenya at the age of two, and again when she was twelve to live for a year in Tanzania, left its imprint. She yearned to see far places, to know other cultures. It was a yearning that led her to her death, at the age of thirty-seven, on a remote volcano in Indonesia. On June 13, 1993, Kelly was fatally injured in a sudden volcanic eruption while climbing Anak Krakatau in the Sunda Strait. My husband and I will forever be haunted by the "what-ifs" implied in the choices we make in life.

This book is dedicated to her: to the shy child who grew up to climb mountains, scuba dive to the ocean's depths, go trekking in Nepal, white water rafting in Suleswesi, sailing in the Caribbean; to the teacher who devoted the last nine years of her life to teaching English to the people of Indonesia; to the beloved daughter who brought joy to the lives of her mother, her father, her brother, sisters, niece and nephew during the thirty-seven years she spent on this planet.

Author's proceeds from this book will go to the Kelly Stephens Memorial Scholarship for Indonesian teachers at Boston University School of Education, established by Robert and Dorothy Stephens in memory of their daughter.

Contents

ACKNOWLEDGEMENTS

My heartfelt thanks to my writer friends who patiently and uncomplainingly read through the many drafts and provided me with valuable feed back on the long road to the completion of this book: Denise Hart, Rachel Hyde, Carol Bistrong, Elisabeth Clark, Rob Dinsmoor, Linda Finigan, Beth Hogan, Elenita Lodge, and Tina Varinos. Also many thanks to Joyce Ross, whose skillful editing polished the text and who suggested some crucial last minute revisions. Most of all I thank my husband, Bob, who understood my need to spend many hours during many years, secluded in my study while I wrote, and who shared this African adventure with me and helped enormously by filling in the gaps when memory failed me.

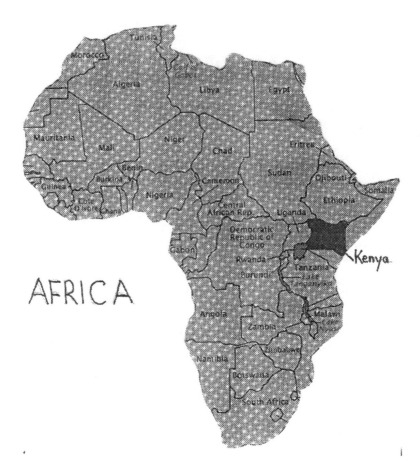

Map of Africa. Map provided by worldatlas.com

Map of Kenya. Map provided by www.worldatlas.com

1

THE JOURNEY BEGINS

I was thirty-three years old the first time I flew over Africa, through darkness so dense the plane might have been hurtling into a black hole in space. When dawn came and the world finally reappeared, the Nile lay far below, a blue thread looping through the desert of southern Sudan before disappearing into the broader blue of Lake Victoria. Soon, the Kenya highlands were sliding beneath us, vast farms that seemed to unroll for miles and Kikuyu villages whose round whitewashed houses and thatched roofs looked as neat as rows of beehives on the steep green ridges. It was November and the jacaranda trees were in bloom. Soft clouds of lavender-blue floated above the ridges and hollows and over the red-tiled roofs of Nairobi. In a moment the wheels of the plane would touch down and my encounter with Africa would begin.

When my husband, Bob, joined the United States Information Agency (USIA) in the mid-1950's, I knew that eventually we would be sent somewhere overseas. To London, maybe? Rome? or Paris?

"But what if I were sent to…New Zealand, for instance?" Bob would sometimes ask. "Would you want to go there?"

"Well, maybe," I'd say. New Zealand—or Australia, or wherever—sounded awfully far away. The farthest I had ever been from where I grew up in New Jersey was Michigan and I lacked his adventurous spirit, or at least I thought I did. Up to then, my world had been small, circumscribed, familiar. My parents' most radical departure from our usual vacation at the Jersey shore had been a week at a Vermont lake one summer when I was ten.

Bob and I never even discussed Kenya. I had recently read *Something of Value* by Robert Ruark, a novel about the Mau Mau uprising against the British colonial government in Kenya, a bloody struggle for independence that had been ravaging the country for the past several years. Ruark described in grisly detail the oaths involving human sacrifice and cannibalism forced by Mau Mau leaders on frightened fellow Africans, and the vengeance of British forces and enraged white

1

settlers who beat, starved, and tortured their African prisoners to gain information about Mau Mau activities. Kenya sounded frightening, a place I never expected or wanted to see.

So when I finished Ruark's book I said to Bob, "You wouldn't expect me and the children to go there…would you?"

But as it turned out, he did. And so did USIA. Bob came home one evening in the fall of 1957 and his first words were, "We have our orders! A two-year tour of duty in Kenya!"

He looked elated. He had been appointed Vice Consul and Cultural Affairs Officer of the United States Information Service in Nairobi (known as the United States Information Agency in the U.S., United States Information Service or USIS overseas.)

"Probably one of the best posts in Africa," he told me. The Mau Mau Emergency was winding down, Nairobi was high and cool so malaria wouldn't be a problem.

"And anyway," he said, "the government will look out for us. Don't worry, we'll be fine!"

I looked at two-year-old Kelly, sitting in her high chair, happily banging her spoon in her mashed potatoes. Cathy and Robbie, eleven and nine, burst out with excited questions. "When do we leave, Dad? Will we fly in an airplane? Will we have to go to school?"

"FINE?" I wanted to shout back at Bob. How could he think we would be fine, taking our children to a place where there were probably all sorts of diseases besides malaria to worry about, never mind the threat of Mau Mau. But like other women of my generation, I had been brought up to believe that my husband's career was all-important, and that it was my job to help and support him, no matter what. The women in my own family, in fact virtually all those I knew, had traveled this road before me. They provided me with a model for how women lived their lives, their identities bound up in their husbands' occupations, the places where they lived dictated by their husbands' jobs. I accepted, almost without question, that where Bob's career took us, we would go. Sometimes I worried vaguely about where that might be, how far away from home, family, and familiar surroundings, but I usually pushed the thought away. It didn't enter my head that my wishes or needs might ever come first.

Now, listening to Cathy and Robbie's eager questions, hearing the excitement in their voices, I knew I didn't want to pass along my anxieties to them. I tucked my visions of steaming malarial jungles, ferocious wild animals, and savage tribes into a far corner of my mind. Pinning my faith on the United States Government, I threw myself into the dizzying preparations for moving a family of five overseas—and tried to believe Bob's optimistic words.

Fortunately, there was so much to do in two short months that I had little time for worrying. I left Kelly with a good friend and neighbor down the street, and while Cathy and Robbie were in school I shopped for footlockers and suitcases, for medicines and toiletries and Christmas gifts, for clothes and shoes to outfit all of us for the next two years.

The clerks in the stores tried to help me. "What size shoe do you think my two-year-old will wear when she's four?" I would ask, and the shoe clerk and I would do our best to guess. According to the State Department's Post Report that Bob brought home, I would need some new clothes myself, like a formal gown, "dressy" suits and dresses, high-heeled shoes, a two-year supply of nylons (no pantyhose in those days.) And skirts and blouses for everyday wear, to replace my usual shirts and slacks. For someone who hates to shop, this was one of the more onerous parts of getting ready. The old Woodward and Lothrop's in downtown Washington, and the Hecht Company in Silver Spring were my salvation. Back then they even had friendly saleswomen who would bring things to the dressing room for you to try on. With their help I was outfitted with a black cocktail dress, a red knitted suit, and other everyday and evening wear.

Sometime during those hectic weeks of preparations, I attended a briefing session for wives going overseas. We were told we would be expected to make calls on other diplomats' wives—the American Ambassador's or Consul General's wife always first, preferably within forty-eight hours of arrival; that we should leave calling cards; that at dinner parties we would seat the most important people according to protocol, at the right of the host and hostess; that we must not offend local people by wearing shorts in public. It all sounded very Victorian and somewhat nonsensical, like something out of Alice in Wonderland's unreal world, but I dutifully packed my proper little black hat, my white gloves, and my new calling cards, and put away my shorts. Unfortunately I learned nothing about Kenya. Mau Mau was not mentioned at all.

Bob, on the other hand, had taken a course at American University on the politics and history of Africa—a general survey of that immense and diverse continent—and had been briefed at the State Department about the current situation in Kenya. At USIS he would be responsible for overseeing cultural and educational activities: advising African students; arranging college scholarships for them in the States; giving English language exams; and organizing official visits of American musicians, actors, dancers, journalists, and athletes.

At night, after the children were in bed, he filled me in as best he could on the history of the British in East Africa, on the workings of the colonial government, and on the names of a few prominent people and the two largest tribes, the Kikuyu and the Luo. The name Tom Mboya was familiar to both of us. He was a young Kenya labor leader who had visited the United States in the fall of 1954, when we saw him interviewed by Dave Garroway on the Today show.

Trying to get my bearings, I pored over the map to find Nairobi, Lake Victoria, the Equator, the port of Mombasa. Still, detailed information about life in Kenya was scanty. No recent pictures of Nairobi were available, nor had we found anyone in Washington who had been there. The State Department's Post Report gave only a meager description of Nairobi and some bare statistics about population and climate. We knew that there were 5,000,000 Africans living in Kenya, 175,000 Asians (meaning people from India), and 65,000 Europeans (a term universally used for all whites, including Americans); that there were two rainy seasons; that most white people had servants; and that our children would attend a European (whites only) school.

Meanwhile, we found an Army doctor and his wife who would rent our house, sent Tammy, our collie, off to Bob's parents in Michigan, and moved Cathy in with Kelly. Cathy's bedroom became the staging area for sorting out four categories of "stuff:" furniture, winter coats, mountains of books to go into storage; suitcases full of clothes and personal belongings to accompany us on the plane; footlockers holding other essentials to be sent via air freight, along with my typewriter and Kelly's crib; and all the rest—children's books and toys, the rest of our clothes, my sewing machine, pictures, a few lamps and favorite chairs, to be crated and shipped by sea.

Somehow everything got done. And even though my house was in a state of semi-chaos, my life turned upside down, my thoughts and feelings a reflection of the turmoil around me, nevertheless, as our departure drew closer, a secret current of excitement occasionally crept through me at the thought of the adventure ahead.

We took off from New York early on a November evening. My mother and father drove in from New Jersey to see us off. I was terrified of flying, especially with three children over three thousand miles of ocean. My only previous flights had been short bumpy ones in pre-jet planes between Michigan and New Jersey, replete with those frequent sickening drops every time the plane hit an air pocket. They hadn't built my confidence in flying. My father, son of a strait-laced Methodist minister and not much of a drinker (nor was I) sensed my anxiety, though I tried hard to hide it. He took me into the bar at the airport while my mother and

Bob entertained the children, and poured a couple of martinis into me. I kissed my parents goodbye a short time later with almost no tears, and in something of a haze, blithely climbed aboard the plane.

My clearest recollection of the first part of the flight was the pilot's announcement over the intercom. "Take a good look down," he said. "Those are the lights of Nantucket, and that's the last bit of the U.S. that you'll see for a while!"

I stared down, my blithe mood gone, my heart plummeting, and wondered if I would ever see the shores of the United States again—or indeed any shore—or if the cold waters of the Atlantic would swallow us all up before morning.

The old DC7C kept lumbering noisily across the ocean, and eventually Cathy and Robbie climbed into their respective berths—the government sent us First Class in those days. They giggled as they squirmed out of their clothes and into pajamas, apparently not daunted, as I was, at the prospect of spending the night in such a cramped dark space. I finally lifted Kelly into my berth, then crawled up beside her and tried vainly to sleep. Bob chose to doze sitting up in his seat. Several times in the night I peered around the curtain and was reassured to see him there, his long legs stretched out into the aisle, his book sliding down in his lap. Keeping vigil while we slept.

During the night and the day that followed, flying in and out of time zones, I lost all track of time and place. Jet lag was a term yet to be invented to describe how I felt. Sunrise seemed to follow on the heels of sunset. Juice, coffee, and rolls appeared at what my head and stomach told me was four o'clock in the morning. We made the necessary refueling stop in Paris, then a short while later it was lunchtime and the Alps were slipping away beneath us, snowy spires gleaming in the afternoon sun. Cathy and Robbie interrupted their coloring long enough to gaze, awestruck, at the sight. In no time at all, the runway in Rome emerged in the dusk.

We spent the night in Rome to rest up for the next part of our long flight to Kenya. The following afternoon we took off again, this time in an old Air France Constellation, propellers thrashing and engines roaring as it droned its way across Africa, fourteen hours without seeing a light except when we stopped to refuel in Libya at Tripoli's King Idris Airport. There, we were herded into the small cinderblock terminal, a lighted oasis in the black void. Outside, dim orange flares stitched the runway. The African night swallowed everything else.

We huddled on cold concrete benches sipping bottles of warm orange squash—that sweet, artificially flavored drink that we would come to know well—and tried to convince our three fretful children that it was an acceptable substitute for Coca Cola. I couldn't blame them for being cranky. I was at a low point myself, here in this godforsaken place in the middle of the night, all of us shivering in the chilly night breeze blowing in from the Libyan desert. Even worse, from my point of view, the captain and crew were lined up at the bar, ordering drinks that were definitely not orange squash.

When we finally reboarded the plane, Kelly lay down with her blond head in my lap and promptly went to sleep. There were no First Class berths on this flight. Robbie sat in front of me, casting frantic looks around the back of his seat each time the elderly woman beside him was airsick. A healthy nine-year-old's need for sleep finally overcame him and he curled up with his head on the armrest and dozed off. Bob, a few rows behind us, was also trying to sleep while near him a baby wailed. Several times he roused himself and came forward to see if I was all right, or walked back to check on Cathy, who had been relegated to the far rear of the cabin. Bob's efforts to have her seated with us in First Class, as she should have been, had elicited only a flood of French and a shrug from the steward. I wondered uneasily what we would do in an emergency, but Cathy took it philosophically. She had admitted to being frightened during the take-off in New York, but now she seemed to relish the chance to pretend she was a worldly young lady, traveling alone.

Throughout the night, as the hours shuddered by, the stewards served a continuous flow of French wines and champagne. Frequently one would carry a tray of filled glasses forward to the cockpit. Unable to sleep, I watched and worried, remembering the grim jokes about "Air Chance," and pondered the improbable fact that I, a housewife fresh from life in a house with a picture window on a street in a Washington suburb, was bound for Africa.

I had grown up in a small New Jersey town in the 1920's and 30's, when there was never to be another war, when the world was safe, life predictable and secure. In my last year of high school, World War II shattered that placid world. Some of the boys in my class enlisted right after Pearl Harbor and were gone before graduation. A few never returned. The war cast a pall over my college years, too, disrupting—or ending—the lives of a whole generation of young men and women. The war, and the Army, brought Bob from Michigan to the Army's Specialized Training Program at Rutgers University, where we met on a blind date. He showed up on a Saturday afternoon, tall, crew cut, studious-looking in glasses, wearing his Michigan State T-shirt—to impress me, he later confessed. We pedaled on bikes to the nearby river, spent the afternoon canoeing, went on to dinner and a movie. By the next afternoon, when we sat by the campus lake holding hands and never stopped talking, it was clear that this was going to be more than a successful blind date. I was still in college when we were married a year and a half later.

During the post-war years Bob went to graduate school on the GI Bill at the University of Michigan and we began raising a family. We lived in Willow Run, in married student housing: flimsy wooden buildings, cold in the Michigan winters, hot in summer, that had been constructed for aircraft workers during the war. We had no hot water, cooked on a wood stove, carried in coal for the living room stove that kept the apartment warm. Without a car, I lugged groceries, wet laundry, and children across the fields in a wagon in summer, on a sled in winter, while Bob rode the bus the fourteen miles to school.

After graduate school, when Bob went to work for USIA, we moved to that suburban house outside Washington. In a row of other houses just like it, with tricycles on the sidewalks and sprinklers whirling on the lawns, it seemed like heaven compared with Willow Run. And now…Africa? During those long hours on the plane, what lay ahead seemed as impenetrable as the black night outside the plane window.

At Nairobi's old Eastleigh airport, a former Royal Air Force base, the plane bumped along a dirt runway, churning up great billows of red dust, and stopped near the cluster of shabby Quonset huts that served as the terminal. We had arrived.

My fears leaped back to life and bunched in a hard cold knot in my stomach. Though the worst of Mau Mau was over, a "State of Emergency" was still in effect. Jomo Kenyatta, alleged leader of the Mau Mau, whom Kenya's Governor Sir Patrick Renison would later call "a leader into darkness and death," was in detention in the far north of Kenya, but the last remaining bands of rebels were still being hunted down in the forests and mountains outside of Nairobi.

I remembered with horror the story that had circulated recently through the State Department and USIA. A European child riding his tricycle in the driveway of his home outside Nairobi had been attacked—and appallingly, unthinkably—beheaded by Mau Mau who sprang from the bushes wielding their *pangas*.

What were we doing here with three children? I wanted to turn around and fly straight home.

Instead, we plunged immediately into a hubbub of arriving and departing passengers, porters, and khaki-clad customs officials. All of them, black and white alike, spoke with a clipped British accent that was hard to understand. They waved us through Customs without even glancing at our bags. Standing outside the gate to greet us were Gordon and Gloria Hagberg from USIS. Their friendly smiles and familiar accents were reassuring, an anchor in the unfamiliar African sea. Gloria, tall, dark-haired, in a yellow shirtwaist dress, took my hand in both of hers and said, "Welcome to Kenya!" I looked into the bluest eyes I had ever seen and felt I had found a friend.

Gloria hurried off to the school where she taught, and the children and I got into the back seat of Gordon's station wagon. While he and Bob helped the porters stow our bags, I studied this man for whom Bob would be working. Shaggy eyebrows, sandy hair turning gray, a rugged face softened by a genial smile as he joked with the porters in Swahili. Again I felt reassured. For the moment, anyway, we were in good hands.

On the drive to the city, I stared out the window at the National Game Park that bordered the road: miles of rolling grasslands studded with dwarfed thorn trees, where lions, zebras, wildebeeste and gazelles roamed, unfenced. Recently, Gordon said, a lion had chased two schoolboys on bicycles along this same road and into the site of the new international airport, just being built. And the previous year a lioness had wandered into the city and sat down on the steps of City Hall. The game wardens tried hard to lure her back to the park but she refused to budge. They finally had to shoot her.

Numb with fatigue, I listened with a mixture of fascination and foreboding. The scenes outside the window began to blur—the grass-covered plain, the trees, the wide African sky all running together like a watercolor left out in the rain. The animals themselves seemed suddenly bizarre: rhinos with horns sticking from their foreheads; giraffes with outlandishly long necks; huge, ungainly ostriches that looked more like fake Disney characters than the real thing.

Beside me, Cathy and Robbie were paying rapt attention to Gordon's stories. They looked intrigued and not at all scared. Bob, his long frame folded into the seat next to Gordon, was staring out the window, absorbed, getting his first look at Africa. Kelly whimpered in my lap. Not even the sight of a giraffe browsing beside the road could divert her. I rocked her back and forth and tried to quiet her fears—and mine.

As we neared the city, bicycle bells competed with honking horns. Trucks, buses, cars, handcarts, bikes, and people streamed around us. Indian mothers in rainbow saris led swarms of solemn dark-eyed children along the roadsides; Indian men in business suits mingled with bearded Sikhs wearing turbans of pale pink or blue. Tall Maasai warriors with mud-smeared hairdos stalked along, naked under blankets slung from one shoulder. Elderly Kikuyu women clad in goatskins, with shining bald heads and masses of wire ornaments and beads, bent over their walking sticks as they plodded along the sidewalks. Some of the younger women wore sari-like *kangas,* the bright colors glowing against the rich earth tones of their skin. Europeans were an occasional pale glimmer in this river of dark faces.

The scene was at once strange and exotic, intriguing and beguiling. I felt curiosity stirring, and some questions. Would I ever find my place in this unfamiliar world? And how would it feel to be one of the privileged minority here?

Gordon dropped us at the rambling old Norfolk Hotel, where we would stay for a few days before moving into our house. The oldest hotel in Nairobi, the Norfolk had opened on Christmas Day in 1904, at the beginning of England's colonial rule in Kenya. Tudor-style, with dark beams crisscrossed on a white-washed exterior, it became the favorite stomping ground of early white settlers. Elspeth Huxley, who wrote *The Flame Trees of Thika* and many other books about Kenya, stayed there with her parents in 1913, on their way to establish their farm at Thika. Travelers, big game hunters, and other white settlers like Karen Blixen, author of *Out of Africa,* often gathered on its veranda to talk, have lunch, drink coffee or scotch—or, in the early years, to engage in the antics that established the Norfolk's reputation as the scene of wild revelry and unconventional behavior.

We would hear many stories of the "old days" while we were in Kenya. Once when Lord Delamere, a well-known early settler, was hosting a party at the Norfolk, he was told by the manager that it was closing time. Delamere locked the unfortunate man in the meat safe with some dead sheep and went on with his party. Other high-spirited guests sometimes celebrated Race Week by throwing each other through the windows, and occasionally the managing director of the Boma Trading Company, a local business, rode his horse right into the Norfolk's dining room and jumped it over the tables. During the Mau Mau Emergency, it was on the veranda of the Norfolk that Robert Ruark gathered atrocity stories from gun-toting settlers for his book, *Something of Value.*

The Norfolk symbolized much of Kenya's early colonial history, but it had long since settled down to a more sedate existence. We would be likelier to meet tourists having coffee on the veranda than colorful Lord Delamere types.

In the courtyard behind the hotel, the roofs of the guest cottages were heavy with masses of purple and orange bougainvillea. Waiters in long white robes and red fezes hurried back and forth with tea trays and clean linens. Bright-colored birds squawked from the palm trees, and beside our door a hibiscus bush bloomed, ablaze with crimson flowers.

I stood on the veranda, the morning sun warming my bare arms. The gray November cold of New York was oceans and continents away. The memory of it was slipping into a past that already seemed part of another life.

We had survived the long flight across half the world.....Maybe we would be all right here, too.

2

THE HOUSE IN MUTHAIGA
AND INVASION OF THE
SAFARI ANTS

Mornings at our house in Muthaiga began with the cooing of doves and soft Kikuyu voices from the road. As we ate our breakfast we could see through the dining room windows the Kikuyu women going by on their way to the forest to gather firewood. They walked briskly, heads high and backs straight, their *kangas* making splashes of yellow and red and green in the early grayness. In late afternoon they passed by again. I would see them no longer brisk or upright, but bent over and plodding under towering bundles of wood, held on their backs by head straps that over the years had worn deep grooves in their foreheads. With their loads of firewood the women trudged back to their villages in the Kikuyu Reserve, where they had cleared patches of forest for *shambas* of millet, maize, sweet potatoes, and beans.

The circular drive in front of our house curved in from the road, hugging a crescent of tall eucalyptus and cedars. In their protective shade, delicate pink frangipani bloomed on gnarled trees, and creamy white gardenias sweetened the air. Behind the house, a forest sloped down to the Mathare River. Even before we moved in, we warned the children that they must never wade there. Innocuous as the little river appeared, we had been told it was infested, like many streams in Kenya, with bilharzia. A parasite carried by river snails, it enters the bodies of bathers through open cuts and sores and invades the liver and other organs. Long exposure had allowed many Africans to build up an immunity, but the disease could be fatal to Europeans. It was one more thing to add to my list of worries.

Our house in Muthaiga

The few days we spent at the Norfolk before moving to the house had been a blur of meeting new people, of cocktail parties and dinners, of Gloria Hagberg scooping up the children to take them swimming or to a movie with a gaggle of American children that included her daughter Paula, who was Cathy's age. Bob started work immediately, and while he settled into a new job, the children and I explored Nairobi. With Kelly in her stroller, we roamed the busy sidewalks of the city. Cathy and Robbie searched in vain for hamburgers and milk shakes. Instead, we poked around in dark little Indian *dukas* on Bazaar Street, where burlap sacks of spices and curry powders crammed the doorways, their aromatic, nose-tickling scents pervading the air. Inside, among brasses and ivories and Chinese silks, we found piles of more prosaic things like uniforms, underwear, towels, and a few novelties too. The children were entranced by some amazing little red coffee beans, no bigger than peas. When a plug was removed, out spilled a dozen tiny ivory elephants, as fragile as microscopic snowflakes.

When our car was shipped up from Mombasa, I took a deep breath and ventured out onto the left side of the road and into the streams of traffic. Dodging bicycles and pedestrians, and with a nervous eye on the lorries and buses, I drove out to Muthaiga School and registered Cathy and Robbie for the January term. Our airfreight arrived, along with Kelly's crib, and we were ready to move from the Norfolk.

We had already arranged to take over the house from another American couple who were leaving, and three servants came with it—a house "boy," an *ayah* (nanny), and a shamba "boy" or gardener. The kitchen "boy"/cook, who worked for the vice consul Bob was replacing, was also looking for a job. Both employers gave the servants good recommendations and urged us to keep them on. Jobs were hard to come by, and these four needed theirs. Marikus, the cook, was saving up for a bride price; Ali, the house boy, sent money home to his wife and little daughter in a village at the coast; Rachel, the *ayah*, paid school fees for her two teenaged children; and the shamba boy, Petro, simply needed work.

Before I came to Kenya, I had vowed I would do without servants. I was used to being alone in my own home and kitchen and doing things my own way, and I was uncomfortable about playing the role of a *"memsahib"*—nor did I know how. I also knew that the cooks, house boys and shamba boys often had to live hundreds of miles from their wives and families, whom they saw perhaps once or twice a year. I objected to the demeaning word "boy" for grown men, and I rebelled at being part of a system that forced families apart.

Almost as soon as I arrived, however, reality changed my mind. Barbara and Mary Claire, the two women for whom the servants had worked, tried to convince me that I would need the help. I would be expected to do my share of entertaining, they said, and I would also be called upon for volunteer work. And besides, said Barbara, "You won't have any of those wonderful modern conveniences like we have at home. No dishwasher, no vacuum cleaner, no automatic washer and dryer, no neat little supermarket packages of plastic-wrapped chicken all cut up and ready to cook. You'd be crazy to try to keep house here without help!"

She was right about the lack of labor saving devices. When I first went to look at our house, I had seen Ali cleaning the tile floors with a broom, a mop, and a square of cardboard for a dustpan, then polishing them by skating around with pieces of sheepskin tied to his feet. In the shipping crate on its way to us from the States was a Sears Wringer Washer—in Ali's eyes, when he saw it, a marvel of modern technology.

"*Hii machini mzuri kabisa!*" he said the first time he used it. This machine is totally good! For the next two years he did the laundry in it every morning on the back porch, a distinct improvement over the usual methods of scrubbing the clothes in the bathtub, or in a stone trough in the back yard.

Clearly we needed the servants and they needed us. I capitulated. The servants stayed. They were happy to be working for Americans. Ali said he had worked for the British before, and he never would again. "Americans—(like washing machines!)—*mzuri kabisa,*" he said.

I knew what he meant about the British settlers. Already I had heard the way some of them spoke to their servants.

"Boy!" they would shout, instead of using the person's name. "*Kuja hapa!* Come here!" They didn't say "please" or "thank you," and made patronizing remarks like, "These people are only just out of the trees, you know!" I couldn't blame Ali for not wanting to work for them.

At one of the first parties we went to, I met a titled Englishwoman who had lived in Kenya for fifty years. When she heard we were Americans, she said: "You Americans! You spoil the Africans rotten. They're cheeky enough already!" She thought we overpaid the servants and were far too indulgent when we let them heat their morning tea on our stove and cook their evening meals in the kitchen when it rained, rather than outside on their little charcoal fires.

Any defense I ventured to offer on behalf of the Africans only increased her outrage. In the end, I bit my lip and kept quiet. Her view of Africans was so far removed from mine that it left no room for dialogue. Unlike me, the white settlers came from a long tradition of colonialism, with all the attitudes toward other races that that implied. In those days Muthaiga, a Nairobi suburb on the edge of one of the African Reserves, embodied that long tradition. It was a European enclave, a world set apart from its surroundings. Housing was strictly segregated. Even the Indian High Commissioner, with the rank of ambassador, had to live in Parklands, the Asian section of town on the other side of the Mathare River. The only Africans in Muthaiga were the servants who stayed in the quarters behind the big European homes. The rest lived in the Reserves or in the African Locations—slums on the outskirts of the city that were like South Africa's Soweto: fly-infested, muddy, without electricity or plumbing, with as many as ten or twelve people jammed into each tiny dark room.

Our servants' quarters were better than most, and unquestionably better than the Locations. They consisted of four cubicles and a communal bathroom, built in a square. Ali's room faced the kitchen door a stone's throw away. The other three opened toward the forest, away from the house. The bathroom had a shower and flush toilet, and all the rooms were lighted with electricity. They were snug and clean—but they were very small, and the contrast between them and our own seven spacious rooms and four baths was enormous—and for me, always disquieting.

I don't know what kind of a house I had been expecting before we came to Kenya. Not a grass hut, of course, but not this handsome house either. Set on five acres of garden and forest, with white stucco walls, black iron balconies, and red-tiled roof, it might have been plucked from a Mediterranean hillside.

But at night, when Ali drew the curtains against the sudden chill after the sun went down, there was no doubt that we were in Africa. All night long the alien voices of the forest hummed and throbbed through the house. I would lie in bed listening to a chorus of insects shrilling and rasping, and to a host of strange hootings and gruntings and high metallic shrieks, accompanied sometimes by what sounded like a leopard's cough.

Sometimes the animals themselves invaded the house. Pale geckoes made forays on the walls, snapping up insects. Bats found their way in and streaked up and down the wide stairwell. Worst of all were the safari ants. We had our first brush with them one night less than a month after we moved into the house. Bob opened the door to go out to a meeting, leaped back in alarm, and slammed the door.

"Safari ants!" he shouted. "Call Ali!"

I raced toward the kitchen. "Ali, *kuja!*" I yelled. "Come!"

Kelly, Robbie, Cathy, Chumley, and I in the garden

Back in the front hall, I crowded up next to Bob and peered out the window. A tide of safari ants was pouring down the driveway, up the front steps, and over the red-tiled stoop, turning it into an undulating sea of reddish-brown bodies. It looked as though the stoop itself were alive.

"Good God!" Bob breathed in my ear.

We stared at the horde in awed fascination. I had seen one of these ants up close in the garden just a day or so before when it marched up the arm of my lawn chair. It was a ferocious looking beast, nearly an inch long, with a seg-mented body and an enormous head from which curved two powerful pincerlike jaws.

Watching them now, some of the stories I had been hearing flashed through my mind, of people being driven out of their homes by ants, of ants attacking small animals and killing them, or devouring larger animals alive. I clutched Bob's arm in alarm. Could this writhing mass, swarming on our doorstep, get up the stairs to the children?

By now Ali had appeared. "*Aieeee! Wadudu mingi sana!*" he cried, looking over my shoulder. Very many insects!

Laughing at our panic, he stepped calmly into the living room, scooped up a shovelful of hot ashes from the fireplace, then opened the front door and sprin-kled the ashes across the sill. The leaders of the ants did an abrupt about-face and headed away. The multitude followed, transforming the driveway into a dark flowing river that vanished into the forest.

A few nights later, on Christmas Eve, I flicked on the bathroom light before going to bed. A red-brown column of ants spilled through the open window, cas-cading down the white bathroom wall and into the tub.

There was no time to call Ali or collect hot ashes. The ants would be out of the tub and all over the floor—and my bare feet—within seconds. My heart jumping wildly, I grabbed the hot water faucet in the tub and turned it on hard. The col-umn of ants, met by the onrush of steaming water, reversed its direction. I watched as it climbed back up the side of the tub, back up the wall, out the win-dow and out of sight.

Thankfully I shut the window, flushed away the bodies of a few drowned ants, and had my bath.

I wasn't in suburban Washington any more. Welcome to Africa.

3

TEA WITH A KIKUYU FAMILY

The night before we left New York, Bob had met Mungai Njoroge, a young Kikuyu medical student who was studying in America. For almost ten years, while attending college and medical school, Mungai had not gone home. The trip would have been prohibitively expensive, but even more importantly, Kenya had been locked in the grip of the Mau Mau uprising and under martial law. Mungai said to Bob, "Who knows what might have happened to me if I had returned home? I could have ended up in jail, or dead—or worse!"

He and the few other Kikuyu students studying abroad during those years lived with anxiety about the consequences of Mau Mau for their country, their tribe, their loved ones, and themselves. Mungai wanted to send messages to his parents, and he urged Bob to call on them as soon as we arrived in Nairobi.

On one of our first Sunday afternoons in Kenya, on our first family excursion outside the city, the Hagbergs drove us to the village of Kikuyu for tea with Mungai's family. Beyond the city the paved road turned to hard-packed red dirt. People thronged the roadsides, waving and shouting "*Jambo!*" as we passed. It was almost impossible to conceive that these same cheerful, friendly people had so recently been ensnared in the unimaginable brutalities of both sides in the Mau Mau rebellion.

The rural scene captivated me: rolling country dotted with flat-topped acacias, soaring eucalyptus, silvery wattles covered with pale gold blossoms, Cape chestnut trees drifting in a pink haze on the horizon. Near the clusters of African huts, stately mangoes spread their dense foliage over deep pools of shade where generations of Kikuyu elders had sat and held their councils.

Was this the Kenya, these the people I had been so afraid of? Already some of my misconceptions were beginning to undergo a major sea change, the specters that had haunted me barely a month ago dissipating.

The Njoroges' farm, a thatch-roofed farmhouse surrounded by banana trees and rich green grass, had been in their family for more than three generations. Rough thorn fences behind the house enclosed flocks of chickens, ducks, pigs, cows, and a donkey. Beyond were the fields where Mrs. Njoroge grew vegetables and Mr. Njoroge raised coffee, for which he had to get special permission from the government.

African farmers in those days were generally prohibited from planting profitable cash crops like coffee, tea, sisal, and pyrethrum, which were permitted on European farms only. The restriction created bitter resentment among many of the African farmers we met. In *Nine Faces of Kenya*, Elspeth Huxley quotes from the autobiography of Harry Thuku, an early African leader who spent nine years in prison in the 1920's for advocating civil disobedience to gain African rights. Under the British, he wrote, he was told he could plant only beans on his land, no coffee. He went on to describe what he did when Uhuru (Freedom) Day came in 1963:

"I was sent a ticket (to the celebration)…but it was very heavy rain at the time, and I could see that many people would be losing their shoes in the mud of the stadium. So I told my wife, 'We shall therefore celebrate our independence by planting our coffee where it is forbidden.'" They planted 15,000 little coffee trees on their land that day, which Thuku considered "a fitting celebration of independence because I had been fighting for Africans to grow coffee ever since 1921."

Mungai's father came to greet us, spare, gray-haired, dignified in a suit and tie, smile lines wrinkling around his eyes and mouth. We shook hands with him and his wife, a thin, friendly little woman in a crisp cotton dress with a white head cloth covering her hair. Speaking very softly in Kikuyu, she beckoned us inside to a combination English/Kikuyu feast spread out on the table. It was the first of many substantial "teas" we would share with hospitable African friends.

Our children gradually became used to eating many unfamiliar foods—roasted goat ribs, Indian curries and *samosas,* English marmite spread on their bread—but that day I was glad to see on the Njoroges' table some foods I knew they would eat: bananas, sandwiches, and scones, alongside the cubes of cold cooked sweet potatoes that I was pretty sure they wouldn't.

Mungai's sister Jemima and her husband Mareka Gecaga had arranged the tea party and drove out from Nairobi to join us. Mareka, a British-trained lawyer employed by a British-owned business firm, had the distinction of being the only African in Kenya at that time with a top position in business. His wife, Jemima, had been among the first Africans recently appointed by the government to the

Legislative Council (Kenya's Parliament), and was its first and only woman member.

This family—the older Njoroges, Mungai, Jemima, and Mareka—was an example of a phenomenon we would witness many times in Kenya: the great leap into the modern world taken by just one generation of Kenyans. The parents were products of their traditional tribal upbringing; the children, though born in a Kikuyu village, made the transition. They were highly educated—Mungai a doctor, Mareka a lawyer, Jemima a legislator—fluent in English and at ease with a Western life-style. I noticed that Jemima and Mareka treated the elder Njoroges with the customary deference, however, and the parents were obviously bursting with pride in the accomplishments of their children.

With the Gecagas' help as translators, Bob delivered Mungai's messages: "Mungai is well and sends greetings. He hopes to be home soon, maybe next year." The parents beamed and thanked him over and over.

In spite of language barriers, there was much talking and laughter as we had our tea and later, when we sat on the grass watching Kelly chase chickens. Bob and I and the two older children had been feeling homesick and keenly aware of the time and distance that separated us from our own parents and grandparents. I felt a rush of warmth for this elderly African couple who had made us so welcome.

When we left, Mr. Njoroge gave a courtly speech in Kikuyu. "You must consider yourselves my children from now on," he told us. "and always welcome in my home." He insisted on giving us one of the chickens. It became the first of our Nairobi flock.

During the next two years we would come to know the Gecagas better and would soon recognize that Jemima's comfortable matronly appearance belied her keen intelligence and political expertise. As a poised and articulate member of Legislative Council, she frequently protested against government policies that ignored the rights of Africans. Tom Mboya once remarked gleefully, "She sounds more like a member of the Opposition than of the government that appointed her!"

Never militant, she spoke in gentle tones and further softened the sting of her vigorous attacks on the government with a warm smile that revealed her prominent teeth.

"A Kikuyu Eleanor Roosevelt," Bob called her affectionately.

Mareka, however, was so British you had to look twice to make sure he was African. He was tall for a Kikuyu, wore handsomely tailored clothes, had a small neat mustache and an impeccable English accent. He seemed, in the words of Gilbert and Sullivan, "the very essence of a proper English gentleman."

Besides being a well-known and respected lawyer, Mareka had a richly-deserved reputation as a scholar, based on the book of Kikuyu tales he had translated into English and the Kikuyu dictionaries he had compiled in both languages. Later, when Bob and I studied Kikuyu, it was Mareka's books that we used.

Over the next few months the Gecagas invited us on a number of family outings with them and their two children. We took a trip to Lake Nakuru, where the water was pink with flamingoes, and spent a Saturday at Gatundu, Jomo Kenyatta's home village, where we attended an African agricultural show, watched a display of tribal dancing, and witnessed a dramatic fire when a banana leaf stall accidentally went up in flames.

One Sunday we picnicked beside a trout stream in Embu, near Mt. Kenya. Jemima took the children fishing, and Mareka, informal for once with his starched shirt collar open and the sleeves of his white shirt rolled up, cut them stalks of sugar cane. "Here is an African treat," he said. "Better than any sweets you can get in a shop!"

The following year, the Njoroge family became the center of a great deal of publicity and excitement when Mungai was featured on the Ralph Edwards TV program, This Is Your Life, as the first Kenyan to graduate with an American medical degree. Each week the show told the life story of a surprise guest, who had no inkling he or she was to be the subject or was about to meet friends, family, teachers, and others from the past. Jemima and the Njoroges were flown to Hollywood to appear on the show.

Afterwards USIS received a file copy and announced a series of public viewings. From all over Nairobi and beyond, Africans flocked to the USIS library to see on the screen this hometown boy who had made good in America. We watched smiles wreathe the faces of Mr. and Mrs. Njoroge when they saw their son again, and enjoyed Mungai's shock and delight at seeing his parents and sister. The elderly couple were as courteous and dignified as ever, Mr. Njoroge in his suit and tie, Mrs. Njoroge still in her cotton dress and headcloth.

I couldn't help wondering what they thought and felt as they were flown over Africa, across Europe and the Atlantic, and on to the American capitol of glitz and glitter, where they were whisked about in limousines, dined in fancy restaurants on strange new foods, and where probably no one but Mungai and Jemima understood a word they said. To their credit, they appeared remarkably unfazed by their foray into that unfamiliar world.

Kelly, Mary Gecaga, and Cathy at the Gatundu Agricultural Show

Kikuyu tribal dancers lining up

Kikuyu tribal dancers

Samburu tribal dancers

Jemima Gecaga at the picnic in Embu

Mareka Gecaga peeling sugar cane

4

GETTING ACQUAINTED WITH KIKUYU WOMEN

In January, Cathy and Robbie started school, and a crew of five African painter *fundis* came with their drop cloths and paint pots to paint our downstairs. *Fundis* were the Mr. Fix-its of Africa, sometimes Africans, more often black-bearded, turbaned Sikhs. When the pipes sprang a leak, we called the plumber *fundi*. If the car broke down, the mechanic *fundi* was summoned. With five painter *fundis* plus four servants, I had nine people in the house. Sometimes, homesick for my own kitchen, for the peaceful daytime solitude of a house with only Kelly and me in it, I yearned to be alone. I often escaped to the garden.

But even there I had company. The patch of forest beyond our garden was thick with underbrush, a haven for snakes and other animals, so in order to create a safer place for the children to play, we had hired a dozen Kikuyu women to clear it. They came to work barefoot, wearing their colorful *kangas*, their shaved heads glistening in the sun. From their ears hung wire hoops the size of saucers, strung with pink and red and blue beads. Their pierced earlobes, stretched wide around wooden disks, were so long they sometimes touched the women's shoulders. I would occasionally see older people, men as well as women, without their earplugs, the long lobes draped handily over the tops of their ears to keep them out of the way.

A few of the women were elderly, the rest young mothers who brought their children along. The older ones, often only four or five years old, had tiny brothers and sisters tied on their backs. While the women worked, the children ran around chasing each other, or had pretend battles with the sticks they helped their mothers collect. The babies watched wide-eyed from the backs of their little nursemaids, often falling asleep in the midst of the games.

For several weeks the women chopped at the bushes with their wide-bladed *pangas*, laughing and chattering as they worked. When I went out into the garden

I would call, "*Jambo!*" and a chorus of "*Jambos!*' would answer. The women seemed friendly and we smiled a lot at each other, but conversation was limited. They spoke Kikuyu, I spoke English, and none of us knew much Swahili.

I felt separated from them by a chasm wider than outer space, a chasm created not just by language but by race, nationality, culture, standard of living—and experience. I had not had to make the terrible choices forced on these women by the still smoldering Mau Mau rebellion. Like all Kikuyu, they had had to either remain loyal to the government and risk torture and death at the hands of the Mau Mau, or take Mau Mau oaths and, if caught, risk the same from government soldiers. Adding another layer of misery to this Hobson's choice was the fact that the women, if they were involved in Mau Mau at all, usually acted only as couriers and suppliers of food to the bands of rebels hiding out in the mountains—bands that often included their own fathers, brothers, husbands, or sons.

I had already noticed a strange phenomenon about Mau Mau. No one talked about it. Even with the horrors so recent, it was as though everyone had come down with a case of total amnesia where Mau Mau was concerned. If referred to at all, it was called "The Emergency" by Africans and Europeans alike. The words Mau Mau were seldom spoken, and neither was the name of its early leader, Jomo Kenyatta. Our African friends rarely volunteered where they had been or what they had done during "The Emergency," and somehow I sensed that I was not to ask. There were rumors whispered about certain people: the European member of the Legislative Council who allegedly had led a patrol that ambushed and killed a Kikuyu chief; the African chief who had been murdered by some of his own tribesmen for remaining loyal to the government. But most of the time it was as though the whole country was in complete denial that something called Mau Mau had ever been, as though in order to put it behind them and heal the awful wounds, they had to pretend it never happened.

The movement nicknamed Mau Mau emerged in the 1940's, the outgrowth of earlier African political associations that had long been pushing for greater rights for Africans and eventual independence for Kenya. Members were recruited from several tribes, but Mau Mau remained largely dominated by the Kikuyu. Jomo Kenyatta, a well-educated Kikuyu politician widely respected by Africans throughout the country, became its leader. Though he consistently counseled against violence and urged peaceful means to achieve independence, he was nevertheless seen as the "evil genius" behind Mau Mau.

In October of 1952 Kenyatta was arrested. The government, under intense pressure from white settlers alarmed by the spread of Mau Mau, put him and nearly two hundred other Kikuyu into detention. On the same day, the "State of Emergency" was declared.

In fact, by the time he was arrested, Kenyatta's influence over younger, more radical members of Mau Mau had waned, and after his arrest they took over. They had already corrupted traditional Kikuyu oaths into "oaths of loyalty" that gradually became more threatening, including pledges "to fight for the African soil that the white man has stolen, and to kill if necessary." Some Kikuyu loyal to the government were killed, and small bands of Mau Mau began raiding outlying European farms, slaughtering the animals and killing a small number of whites (thirty-two, according to the recent book, *Imperial Reckoning*, by Caroline Elkins.) The violence continued to escalate, and by the time we arrived in Kenya in 1957, although very few whites had died, thousands of Kikuyu had been killed by government forces and many more thousands had been put in detention or sent back to the Kikuyu Reserves. (Caroline Elkins estimates that 50,000 were killed and 320,000 put in detention.) The Mau Mau Emergency may have been coming to an end, but as we would see, the changes it brought about were only beginning.

A strange metamorphosis would occur in the public perception of Jomo Kenyatta, whose very name was anathema in 1957 and who, almost certainly unfairly, was blamed for the worst atrocities of Mau Mau. When he was released from prison in 1961, he became the respected representative of his people and negotiated with the British for Kenya's independence. Later it was hard to imagine this majestic, dignified figure, who after independence counseled tolerance and forgiveness between whites and blacks, as the alleged ruthless leader behind the cruel deeds of Mau Mau.

I knew little of this back in 1957. It was only through reading later accounts that I was able to piece it all together. But I did know enough to realize that I couldn't even begin to imagine what the Kikuyu women clearing our forest must have endured in the preceding few years. Nevertheless, I felt a bond with them. They were women, wives, mothers like me. Surely we had some of the same feelings and anxieties. Without a common language, though, we would probably never be able to share them.

One day, however, I saw our shared maternal feelings clearly demonstrated. Kelly was playing in the garden, her doll propped in the sandbox beside her. Two of the women came out of the forest and stood looking at the doll, pointing and speaking in rapid Kikuyu. Soon the other women joined them, gathering in a ring around Kelly, their eyes on the doll, their hands reaching out. Obediently Kelly handed the doll over while I stood by watching, wondering what was going to happen. The women took turns cuddling the doll, rocking it, poking at its blue eyes and caressing the blond hair as they passed it around from one to another. Kelly's anxious gaze followed the doll from hand to hand until, smiling and still jabbering in Kikuyu, one of the women finally gave it back.

Another day one of them approached as I was cutting flowers for the house. In her garble of Swahili and Kikuyu I made out the Swahili words for "head" and "bad." I guessed from her gestures and expression that she had a headache, so I gave her two aspirin. Next day, all smiles, she presented me with a basket of African sweet potatoes. I cooked some for dinner that night. Pale yellow and delicious, they were like a cross between our American white and sweet potatoes.

She obviously passed the word that I had good medicine, because after that the women came to me with all their ailments—mostly scratches and small cuts from their pangas that I easily doctored with iodine and bandages, the way I did with my own children.

As I tended to a cut leg one day, my patient reached out to finger the embroidered black cotton skirt I was wearing. Chattering in Kikuyu, she kept plucking at it. I caught the words "*shillingi moja.*" One shilling. She wanted to buy my skirt for fourteen cents!

I've always been sorry I didn't let her have it. I had others in my closet, after all. But without stopping to think, I smiled at her and shook my head. "*Hapana,* Mama," I said.

With a shrug and a high shrill giggle that I took to mean "no hard feelings," she picked up her panga and went back to work.

Weeks later, when the work was finished and the women had taken their *pangas,* their children and their huge head loads of underbrush back to the Reserve, the empty forest rang with unaccustomed silence. I had the garden to myself again but now, perversely, I missed the chatter and laughter, the cheerful company of the women.

5

WHITE SETTLERS AND A MIDNIGHT COLD BUFFET

Just beyond our house in Muthaiga the road began its ascent to the little settlement at Limuru, climbing almost three thousand feet over a distance of only twelve miles into a high, cool, often misty world. We began making the trip frequently, to visit some of the new American and English friends we had met, or to dine at the Farm Hotel, run by a French couple, where I ate my first artichokes, gnocchi, and escargots. Sometimes on a Sunday we drove up for high tea at the Brackenhurst, a hotel so typically English it looked as though it belonged in a village in Devon. An open fire warmed a dining room cozy with copper pots and geraniums, and at teatime waiters wheeled in trolleys laden with a lavish assortment of jam tarts, scones, rich pastries and cakes. It was Robbie's idea of heaven. For his tenth birthday, he chose tea at the Brackenhurst with four of his friends.

Along the road to Limuru, Africans on bicycles and on foot poured in both directions, carrying loads of firewood, charcoal, or vegetables. Every few miles we would pass long lines of people waiting patiently at police checkpoints to show the hated passbooks that all Africans had to carry whenever they moved between the countryside and city.

Halfway to Limuru was Banana Hill, a large Kikuyu settlement where row upon row of round thatched houses terraced the hillsides. The broad leaves of banana trees waved from every dooryard, and smoke from a hundred cook fires filled the air. In stalls beside the road, women sold baskets and fruit and bark cloth mats. When we occasionally stopped to buy bananas, the women seemed friendly enough, but the men lounging nearby did not. Their unsmiling faces and hostile stares were reminders of the rumors we had heard, that in the early years of Mau Mau its radical young leaders had their headquarters here.

Often, before the gray mists of Limuru closed in, we would stop the car and turn to look down on the vast chunk of Kenya that lay at our feet. The green ridges of Kikuyuland unfurled below. Far-off were the man-made cityshapes of Nairobi, and beyond them, to the south and east, the dry plains that dropped gradually down to the sea, three hundred miles away. To the west, just visible, were the dark blue peaks of the Ngong Hills. In the high thin air at eight thousand feet, I would feel as though I were perched on the very top of the world and might any moment sail off like a giant bird.

Coming back from Limuru at night, wrapped in fog and with no lights anywhere except the headlights of our car, I would have the eerie sensation of hurtling blindly through space. Even when we left the mists behind and the world reappeared, only the stars divided the night sky from the earth—except for the scattering of lights that was Nairobi, tiny pinpricks on the invisible plain.

Toward the end of January we received an invitation to dinner from our landlord, an Englishman with a hyphenated name who lived in Limuru. Coming as it did from an old Kenya settler, this friendly overture surprised us. Most settlers were skeptical of Americans, whom they suspected, often rightly, of sympathizing with the Africans.

White settlers like Mr.W-N had been in East Africa for about fifty years. Before that, during the second half of the 19th century, explorers and missionaries like David Livingstone had charted the interior of this little known continent, and in 1885 at the Congress of Berlin (a gathering of European powers; no Africans were consulted) East Africa was divided up and arbitrary boundaries drawn. The area later called Kenya went to the British, Tanganyika to the Germans.

The settlers from Britain and South Africa who began to arrive around the turn of the century were drawn to Kenya by the prospect of free land, or the lure of exotic surroundings, or the hope of better opportunities than they had at home. They enjoyed the kind of life Kenya offered: cheap labor, including servants; a beneficent climate; an abundance of game in a setting of singular beauty; and freedom from much of the government regulation back home. As I had already learned, they brought with them the attitudes and expectations of the long British tradition of colonialism, and the goal of creating an eventually self-governing "white man's country" like Australia, New Zealand, and South Africa. Little thought was given to the rights or role of the native peoples of Kenya.

The Africans, and especially the Kikuyu, chafed under the decades of white government that followed, and the restrictions imposed on them: denial of the vote, the woeful lack of schools for Africans, the requirement to carry a passbook, the hut taxes they had to pay. (Taxation without representation was not an exclusively American colonial problem.) Most of all, the loss of their land to white settlers festered in the hearts of the Kikuyu. Some of the land had been "bought" from Africans who were under the impression that they were merely "loaning" or giving temporary rights to the land, as was their custom. Other lands were simply taken.

From the beginning the white settlers' views and those of the Colonial Office back in Britain differed widely. The Colonial Office, or at least some individuals within it, felt a responsibility over the years to protect the rights of Africans, and they opposed self-government by the settlers. Winston Churchill expressed their viewpoint in 1908 when he said, after visiting East Africa,

"It will be an ill day for these native races when their fortunes are removed from the impartial and august administration of the Crown and abandoned to the fierce self-interest of a small white population."

For a long while, this seemed in danger of happening. Not until 1944 was the first African appointed to the Legislative Council to represent his people, and it was another thirteen years, in the wake of Mau Mau, before the first African members were elected. The "land question" was still not resolved. Land in the "White Highlands," which had formerly belonged to the Kikuyu, as well as Maasai grazing land in the Rift Valley, continued to be reserved strictly for whites.

By the time the Mau Mau rebellion broke out, the privileged life led by the settlers had virtually disappeared for most Britons back home. In East Africa, second and third generation settlers clung to it. Isolated on widely scattered farms, they came together on weekends for their sunuppers and sundowners, their curry lunches and polo matches, their cricket and their horse races. With a phone system that ranged from unreliable to nonexistent, the settlers depended on their weekend get-togethers for news and gossip from other farms and from Nairobi.

As the threat of Mau Mau increased, the tight white circle had closed ever more protectively. White farmers were a tiny minority in a hostile environment, among millions of Africans. Increasingly, armed with guns, they sealed themselves off behind locked doors. Only with other whites did they feel safe, and even some of those—such as Americans—they distrusted.

Their colonial sensitivities had been heightened after World War II when the American government had urged the end of colonialism around the world. They interpreted the presence of Americans in Kenya as evidence that we were there to encourage, if not foment, African independence. They saw us as a threat, whereas we believed we were there to help with the monumental task of preparing for the inevitable approach of independence.

We saw proof of their suspicions almost daily in the press and in remarks in the Legislative Council. Editorials, letters to the editor, parliamentary speeches frequently questioned the U.S. role in Kenya. Their theme, with some variations, was always, "What are the Americans up to now?"

It was common knowledge that the movements of Tom Mboya and other African leaders were carefully watched, and probably their visits to our house were documented. Even the most innocent contacts between Americans and Africans were sometimes misinterpreted. Gordon Hagberg happened to be at the airport one night, seeing a friend off, when Tom Mboya arrived on an incoming flight. They shook hands, exchanged a few words, and each went his own way.

Headlines in the East African Standard the next day proclaimed: "Head of American Agency Meets Tom Mboya." A hullabaloo ensued. Questions were raised in Legislative Council, and some of the Members suggested that the Government request Gordon's withdrawal from Kenya. That didn't happen, but the fuss that was raised over this brief chance encounter was indicative of how wary the settlers were of our presence in Kenya.

We were consequently not only surprised but pleased to accept the invitation from our landlord, and looked forward, though with some trepidation, to what we thought would be an interesting evening. Our invitation had indicated that this was to be a costume party. We were still living with only the contents of our suitcases and airfreight, in a partially furnished house, waiting for our sea freight to arrive, so I didn't have much to work with. In the end I went as what I was: an American in Kenya, wearing a black cocktail dress with the first gardenia from our garden pinned to the shoulder, and an embroidered wool stole, for which I was later thankful, wrapped around my shoulders. Bob, as a northern Michigan lumberjack, wore a borrowed plaid shirt, red cap and boots, and carried an axe.

I don't remember what most of the guests wore, though I have a dim recollection of a mustached cowboy in a bandana and ten-gallon hat, two women in short flapper dresses and long strings of beads, and a strapping fellow whose hairy red knees peeked from under a Scottish kilt. None of them seemed to be feeling the cold here in Limuru the way I was. Icy fingers of mist seeped in around doors and windows and for some incomprehensible reason, no fires burned on the generous hearths.

We were the only Americans present, in fact the only ones from the diplomatic corps. All the other guests came from surrounding farms, and all knew each other. The damp chill in the house was matched by their coldness toward us. No one talked to us. I felt as though the mist had rendered us invisible. When we tried to initiate conversations people mumbled a vague yes or no, not meeting our eyes, and wandered away. Our host, busy trading stories with a knot of old cronies, paid us scant attention, but his daughter at last took pity on us. Seating herself beside me in a row of chairs along the wall, she said brightly, "Do tell me all about America!"

I smiled at her, grateful for this friendly overture, but before I could get started she was deep in conversation with a friend who had come along—something about horses—and I was forgotten.

Smiling hopefully and circulating around the room, Bob and I shivered our way through the hours and consoled ourselves with thoughts of the hot meal that must surely be served soon. We were beginning to get accustomed to late dining in Nairobi. It was not unusual to have dinner at ten o'clock at night. But this meal turned out to be a midnight supper—and to our horror, a cold buffet!

Teeth chattering, we surveyed the platters of cold meats, cold pickled beets, cold beans and carrots, cold potatoes, cold rolls, everything cold, cold, cold. The thought crossed my mind that the British must get some kind of masochistic pleasure out of pushing the limits of physical discomfort. Why else would they want to eat cold boiled vegetables at midnight on a raw wet night? Oh well, I thought, at least there'll be hot coffee. But no. Only Scotch and soda. No ice.

Bob and I laugh about it now, but the dinner in Limuru was without doubt one of the most physically uncomfortable and socially frustrating experiences of our two years in Kenya. The people that night seemed to personify the typical settler attitude towards Americans: somewhere between indifference and outright antagonism.

But not all settlers we met were like that. A couple of weeks later we were invited to the birthday party of our neighbor, Mrs. Cecily Pitt-Moore. On her many-acred estate among mossy fish ponds, tinkling waterfalls, and meticulously terraced gardens, we met two elderly Englishwomen and longtime Kenya residents. I listened with fascination as, friendly and comfortably dowdy in their cardigans and tweeds, they talked of "the old days" when Nairobi was a dusty frontier railhead, and settlers rode in bullock carts and rickshas. They remembered Berkeley Cole and Denys Finch Hatton and Karen Blixen.

"Her house is still there—out in Karen, you know," one of them said, and told me how to find it. I had the eerie sensation of meeting characters who had stepped live from the pages of the book I was reading: *Out of Africa* by Karen Blixen, the now-famous story of the years she spent early in the twentieth century on her coffee farm in Kenya. Her life in Africa had seemed part of another, long-ago era, and yet…here were two women who had known her.

Everyone at Mrs. Pitt-Moore's party that night was a long-time white resident of Kenya except ourselves. Later that same night we went on to a party at the home of our friend, Dr. Samson Mwathi, where again, everyone was a long-time black resident of Kenya except us. We were never long without reminders of Kenya's contrasts—and deep divides.

The African party was a noisy, cheerful affair held in the bare, cement-floored courtyard of Dr. Mwathi's home. Like all Africans, he lived in one of the Locations, though his home was considerably larger than most, a series of small rooms opening onto the square inner courtyard. The party was a celebration of the departure of several young Kenyans for college in America. Few African women were present. I remember only Dr. Mwathi's wife Jambe and a shy young woman who was one of the departing students. I tried in vain to draw her out, to tell her about the United States and ask if she had any questions I might be able to answer, but she answered only in monosyllables. I feared for her, and the culture shock that lay in wait. In fact, as it turned out, almost every Kenyan whom Bob was later able to track, including the few women, did exceedingly well in their colleges and universities, made countless friends in America, and returned home to help run their country after Independence. I needn't have worried.

The next year, at the Coast on holiday, we met another settler family, the Scott-Smiths from Southern Rhodesia, who occupied a cottage near ours. Friendly and outgoing, they exhibited a refreshing lack of hostility and suspicion towards Americans and went out of their way to invite us to join them for dinner or go snorkeling and swimming with their children and ours. Congenial as they were, though, we had to skirt carefully the subject of race after a few strained conversations when our differing views became glaringly apparent. When we mentioned African friends like Tom Mboya and their desire to have a voice in their government, the Scott-Smiths reacted with an odd kind of rationalization. That was fine for Kenya, they said, but Africans in Kenya were different. Rhodesian Africans were hopeless—lazy and insolent and totally useless without the whites. Ironically, these were the same kinds of things we had heard Kenyan settlers say about Kenyan Africans.

This was an uncomfortable situation. Faith and Scotty's convictions were strong and deeply held. Like some of the people we had met in Nairobi, they were not likely to be swayed by any arguments of ours. And yet we liked them. They were unpretentious, hearty, and forthright, reminding us of mid-westerners from America's farm states. Their heritage was similar: sturdy, adventurous pioneer stock, like the Americans who settled the West. Their forebears, too, had traveled through an unmapped wilderness by covered wagon, crossing blazing deserts and menacing streams, defying the threat of savage animals and hostile tribes, to establish homesteads in the interior. Faith Scott-Smith's grandparents

had trekked to Rhodesia from South Africa, had cleared land for a farm and settled down to raise a family. Faith said her father was the second white baby to be
born in Rhodesia.

"When the baby—my father—became ill," she went on, "my grandmother
picked him up and walked three hundred miles to the coast, through jungle and
forest, to get medical help."

These were tough people. We couldn't help admiring their spirit, even while
we regretted that blind spot about race that erected an invisible wall between us.

For a few years we exchanged Christmas cards and notes with Faith and
Scotty. Theirs were full of bitter laments about the long struggle between Rhodesia's Africans and the white settler government. Finally, in 1980, as a result of
international sanctions and a decade of guerrilla warfare, Robert Mugabe became
the first African Prime Minister. Rhodesia's white settlers were faced with the
same choice as those in Kenya: live under an African government, or leave.

In one of our own moves we lost touch with the Scott-Smiths, and I don't
suppose we will ever know which option they chose: to stay in the new country of
Zimbabwe, or emigrate to Australia or New Zealand—or South Africa, where a
similar chain of events would later unfold.

6

OUR EXTENDED FAMILY: ALI, RACHEL, AND MARIKUS

With so many servants and the two older children in school, I sometimes felt robbed of my identity. Most of my usual roles—cook, housekeeper, laundress, gardener—had been taken over by others and I had few new ones yet to replace them. Bob had plunged enthusiastically into his new job. He enjoyed working for Gordon, free of the cumbersome bureaucracy of Washington, where he had felt like a human cog in a huge machine. Here, he was meeting an exotic mix of people of all races in the heady atmosphere of Nairobi, with all its new and exciting sights and smells and sounds. Here too, he felt his work could make a difference, that it could have a direct impact on the lives of some of the people with whom he was developing face-to-face relationships, particularly students thirsty for higher education.

I was the wife and mother who had come along for the ride. Some mornings I would survey the empty hours ahead and wonder how to fill them. The role of memsahib that had been thrust upon me was ill defined, and one I continued to feel uncomfortable with, like someone trying to squeeze into another's clothes. I hated giving the servants orders, so except for periodic hassles involving Marikus, I left them on their own as much as possible. Luckily, thanks to their previous memsahibs, they all seemed to know their jobs. Sometimes I wondered if the household would just continue to run along smoothly without me, should I suddenly disappear.

The few new duties I had, as hostess, head cook, and chauffeur, took up only part of my time. Mornings, after breakfast, I drove the children the three miles down the road to Muthaiga School, picked them up at one o'clock for lunch, drove them back for the afternoon session at two, fetched them again at four. Kelly rode along with me and kept me company when I had errands to run. Usually in the late morning she went for a walk with Rachel, or played in the garden while I watched over her and read, feeling guilty and decadent for sitting around in the morning while four other people worked.

Most days, while the servants had their two hours off in the afternoon and Kelly napped, I relished the silence in the house. I read, wrote my weekly letters to our parents, or sewed new clothes to replace the ones the children were already outgrowing. Robbie's legs seemed to get longer daily, and Cathy was shooting up, changing into a pre-teenager before my eyes.

January is the beginning of summer in Nairobi, the hot season, so when the children came home from school I often took them swimming in a local pool. Sometimes instead they played in the garden, which was frequently filled with kids—neighborhood children, and later, as we met more people, those of other American, English, Asian, or African friends. The long expanse of grass in the side garden, the shady forest sloping toward the river, gave them plenty of space for running, hiding, or their favorite past-time—swinging out over the hillside on a long vine that hung from one of the trees.

Robbie and his friends made a fort in the forest out of the crate our car came in, and we found a fundi to build a sandbox for Kelly with some of the leftover lumber. Often we had extra children for dinner, or to spend the night, or Cathy and Robbie were invited to do the same at a friend's house.

Africans in Kenya seemed to universally love children, and the servants made a big fuss over ours, especially Kelly. But Marikus's loud voice frightened her, and it was a few weeks before she really warmed up to Ali and Rachel. Being suddenly plopped down in Africa at the age of two had not been easy for her. She was a shy child, quiet and content anywhere so long as she could stay close by my side or Cathy's or Bob's, but reluctant to be left with anyone else, even friends and grandparents back home in the States. Her first close contact with Africa, on our first day at the Norfolk, had been traumatic. I had gone outside to wander around the courtyard with Cathy and Robbie while we waited for Kelly to wake up from her nap. Suddenly her screams shattered the afternoon quiet. She had opened her eyes to find an unfamiliar face, topped by a strange-looking red fez, bending over her as the room boy adjusted a mosquito net over her bed. He had left the room on a wave of Swahili, smiling apologetically, while I gathered her up in my arms and tried to comfort her. It was a long time before she stopped crying.

For a while, after we moved into the house, Kelly came out of her room each morning and greeted Ali and Rachel with a friendly "*Jambo*," and at bedtime solemnly shook their hands when she said goodnight, but she was highly resistant to letting Rachel do anything for her. She was quickly becoming bilingual and soon knew far more Swahili than any of us. When Rachel suggested that it was time for a bath or a walk, Kelly would often burst out with a string of Swahili whose message was something like, "NO WALK, NO BATH, NO RACHEL! *KWENDA!* (GO AWAY!)"

I would look at Rachel apologetically, but she would shrug and say, "Kelly *kali sana leo!*" meaning 'Kelly is very cross today.' Her face would crinkle with laughter. Not much could shake her composure, even when Kelly exhibited these symptoms of the Terrible Twos. The turning point came the day Kelly went to the back door and called, "Rachel, come. Go for walk now!" From then on Rachel was an integral part of Kelly's small circle of favorite people.

For those first few weeks, I followed Ali and Marikus around, English-Swahili dictionary in hand, and tried to learn as much of this East African lingua franca as I could. It is a lilting, musical language, pleasant to the ear, but the grammar is complex. It has many different verb tenses, classes of nouns, and forms of address. The best I ever achieved was a rudimentary "Kitchen Swahili."

Rachel claimed not to understand English (though I suspected she did) so sometimes when my limited Swahili failed me, we enlisted Ali to translate. The only adult women in a houseful of men, we shared an interest in the things women like to talk about: our families and our homes—hers two hundred miles away in Nyanza Province near Lake Victoria in western Kenya, mine thousands of miles away in the States. She examined with interest the pictures on Kelly's bureau of my mother and father, and when she saw me writing a letter home, always asked that I send her greetings to "Mama Mzee and Baba"—Old Mother and Grandfather.

Rachel cleaned Kelly's room, washed and ironed her clothes, and baby-sat with all three children when Bob and I went out in the evening. After the children were in bed, she dozed by the living room fire until we got home. There was a solid dependability about her that led me to trust her right from the start.

In her morning garb of crisp blue uniform and white head cloth, or all in white after her two hours off in the afternoon, she was always immaculate. She walked with calm dignity, back straight and head high from the years of carrying head loads since she was a child. One day I saw her coming home, bearing herself like a queen, but instead of a crown she carried a huge slab of stone on her head, balancing it as easily as a feather pillow. "*Kwa chua mahindi,*" she told me. For grinding corn.

My husband, Bob

Cathy, Robbie, and Kelly in our living room

Cathy and Robbie, with Chumley, on the garden wall

Rachel and Kelly set out for a walk.

Rachel and Kelly on Karura Avenue

A Luhya, from one of Kenya's smaller tribes, Rachel had been raised by a missionary couple, the Ludwigs, at an upcountry American mission in Nyanza, had married and had two daughters and a son. The oldest, a married daughter, lived upcountry. The other daughter, Filois, attended a school run by the Ludwigs, the same people who had raised Rachel and who had been transferred to a school near Nairobi. Rachel's son Green was away at boarding school in Uganda, a full day's bus ride from Nairobi. We met both children when they came to spend the semester break with their mother in Muthaiga. Filois was about fourteen, a plump, pleasant-looking girl, soft-voiced and shy. Green, a few years older, bore an uncanny resemblance to his mother. Both children were polite and well behaved, a pleasure to have around.

Rachel never talked about her husband, but I learned about him from Mrs. Ludwig when we took Filois back to school after the break. The Ludwigs had been in Kenya for thirty-one years and had known Rachel since she had come as a small girl to board at their school. After she left school and married, she stayed on with the Ludwigs to cook and keep house. Her three children were born while she was with them.

"Then," said Mrs. Ludwig, shaking her head indignantly and setting her chins quivering, "Rachel's husband married a second wife. Rachel was a Christian, and she was heartbroken. I remember how she cried and cried. She refused to live with her husband after that. She told him she would get by on her own. And she did!"

I was not surprised. I had already sensed the solid core of strength and quiet determination that lay beneath Rachel's serene exterior, but now I knew at what emotional cost it had come. My heart ached for the young Rachel, caught in the cultural conflicts that Christian missionaries had often introduced to a society traditionally based on polygamy.

Rachel continued to work for the Ludwigs, and later as an ayah for several families in Nairobi. She earned enough money to pay school fees for all three of her children.

Sometimes a well-dressed, handsome man rode out to Muthaiga on his bike to visit her. I would see his bike leaning against the wall outside her door, or glimpse them sitting and talking on her step. I asked her one day who he was.

"*Rafiki yangu* (my friend), memsahib," she answered, and that was all I ever found out.

She was not only an excellent ayah, but an enterprising businesswoman as well. With Ali's help she began clearing a plot behind the quarters for a shamba. Some of the vegetables she raised went into the fish soups and chicken stews that she shared with Ali, but the rest she sold to other Africans. And she was soon conducting a brisk business in ballpoint pens. She had somehow found out where she could order them wholesale, and she had them delivered to Bob's office. There was no home delivery of mail in Kenya then, nor is there now. People who can afford it have boxes at the post office and collect their mail themselves. All of our mail, and that of the servants, came to the Consulate and Bob brought it home at lunchtime. When the pens arrived, Rachel would resell them at a profit to other African servants in the neighborhood. She had created a demand for pens as status symbols among people who couldn't write!

In spite of Rachel and Ali's friendly relationship, it didn't take me long to realize that there was friction in our midst. The easy, laughing exchanges between them would change to cool politeness when Marikus appeared. He argued endlessly with the other servants about the most trivial matters, his abrasive voice getting on everyone's nerves, including mine. He also, not long after our bout with the safari ants, embroiled us in another African-style crisis. It was to set a pattern for our two-year relationship with him. He seemed born to live out Murphy's Law.

One evening after dinner he came to Bob and me and said that after months of negotiations, he had finally paid the bride price of one hundred fifty shillings and two cows for a wife. He asked our permission to bring his new wife to Nairobi. We knew wives were not supposed to live in the servants' quarters, but we agreed to let Joyce come for what we believed would be a short visit.

Like Marikus, she was a Luo, Kenya's second largest tribe, from the area around Lake Victoria. She arrived by bus a few days later: a big awkward girl in a shapeless cotton dress who spoke little and smiled even less. With Marikus busy in the house, she spent her days sitting in the sun on the step outside his room. I thought she might be lonely and homesick and tried several times to talk to her in my limited Swahili, but she wouldn't look at me and just hung her head, not answering. Only when the children came to play near the quarters did she show any animation. She would smile then, and toss a ball back and forth with Kelly, but she rarely spoke.

Her one great accomplishment was the unusual way she smoked. As she sat on the sunny step, she would flip the lighted end of her cigarette inside her mouth, then with a quick twist of tongue and lips flip it quickly out again, blowing smoke rings into the air. The children would gather around and watch, fascinated, as Joyce sat silently smoking and flipping.

A few days after she arrived, a great commotion broke out in the quarters. Marikus burst into the living room where Bob and I sat drinking tea.

"*Bwana, bwana,*" he cried. "I'm sorry, bwana, memsahib, excuse me, but they have taken Joycie away!"

"What do you mean, Marikus? Who is 'they'?" Bob asked.

"Joycie's brothers, they have taken her down to the Locations. They say I have not paid the bride price, and that I still owe some shillings and one cow, so they have taken her back. It's not true, bwana, I paid. I sent the one hundred fifty shillings and the two cows and I owe her father nothing. You must help me!" His eyes turned frantically from Bob to me.

"All right, Marikus, calm down," said Bob. "Do you know where they've taken her?"

"Yes, bwana, to Kariokor Location, where her brothers live."

"Well, come on, we'll go have a look." To me Bob said, "I'll drive him down there and try to find out what's going on."

"Please be careful," I said. "Are you going to the police?"

"I guess I'll have to," he sighed. "We'll be back soon—I hope."

With Marikus in the front seat twisting his hands and moaning, Bob drove off in the jeep. Later I learned what happened. Leaving Muthaiga's smooth tarmac roads, they had approached the African Locations on the eastern edge of the city. The suburban homes in their gardens of bougainvillea and hibiscus gave way to empty fields and rows of low tin-roofed buildings separated by muddy lanes. Children playing on the bare patches of earth froze, wide-eyed, at the sight of a white man.

Marikus had directed Bob to the police station, a bungalow surrounded by a neat border of white-washed stones and plantings of bougainvillea. The two African *askaris* (policemen) listened to Marikus's hysterical outburst, then one of them spoke to him in Swahili. The other turned to Bob. "We will go with you, bwana, to look for this man's wife."

They all got into the jeep and drove a short distance, then stopped outside one of the doors. The English-speaking askari again turned to Bob. "You will please stay here. If there is trouble, it will be better if you are not with us." One of the askaris knocked and the three men disappeared inside. Bob could hear loud voices shouting in a jumble of Swahili and Luo. Marikus's high, frenzied tones rose above the rest.

The argument dragged on until finally the askaris came out with Joyce between them. As she walked past Bob, he could see the glowing end of her cigarette disappearing and reappearing in the dark. She was followed by an exhausted-looking Marikus.

Silent as ever, Joyce had climbed into the jeep. The three men climbed in after her.

"What happened?" Bob asked as they drove back toward the police station.

One of the askaris answered. "This woman's father sent word to her brothers here in Nairobi that he wanted more bride price. He is asking for one more cow and fifty additional shillings. But we have decided that since this man here has already paid the agreed-upon price, the woman belongs with him."

So Joyce came home with Marikus and resumed her life of sitting on the step and smoking. Whether she had wanted to come back, whether she was content with her fate, or just resigned, I would never know. Nor could I guess what her relationship was with Marikus. Had it been an arranged marriage? A love match? Had Marikus's agitation over her disappearance been solely about the possible economic loss, or did he really care for her? To my eyes, Joyce was not an attractive girl, nor did she ever show any initiative or energy, or even interest in anything. She and their relationship remained an enigma.

The whole question of bride price and the negotiations surrounding it were an enigma too. How was a young woman's worth decided? How many cows, how many shillings for a comely seventeen-year-old, for example, as opposed to a less attractive woman of twenty-five or thirty? And less attractive in whose eyes? What were the African standards of beauty, or didn't beauty count? Maybe strong muscles and good teeth were a greater asset. In older women age was respected and an ample figure admired, but I suspected that for younger women the standards were different.

The idea of attaching a price to a prospective bride was repugnant to me, though I understood it was often viewed more as marriage insurance, a guarantee that the woman would not be ill-treated lest she return to her father and the price the husband had paid be forfeited. It was also insurance that the woman would fulfill her duties so her father would not have to return the bride price. Still, it seemed too much a commercial transaction, the buying and selling of a piece of merchandise rather than marriage the way I viewed it, as the coming together of two human beings.

Marikus worried that Joyce's father would continue to demand an additional bride price, or try to take her back. For many days he didn't smile, and I could hear dark mutterings from the kitchen. But though there were no more demands and no further attempts to kidnap Joyce, a new mini-crisis involving Marikus was about to erupt.

I had noticed that our tea, sugar, flour, and oil were beginning to disappear rather fast. They were kept in the "locked store," a pantry enclosed by grillwork with a padlock on the door. It was meant to prevent pilfering, but I was reluctant to live in a kitchen with locked doors and go around with keys jingling at my belt. So most of the time the "store" remained open.

One morning Ali came to me, an uncharacteristically worried look on his face. "Memsahib!" he said. "Marikus is taking the things from the store—*sucari, chai,* (sugar, tea)…You lock it, memsahib! Lock the store!"

I felt we provided generously for the servants. In addition to their pay, they had their own rations of tea, sugar, oil, *posho,* and meat, which I bought every week when I went marketing. They also got a tetrapak of milk delivered with our supply each morning as well as an occasional chicken and a bag of charcoal every month. The posho, like a coarse cornmeal, was their staple. They made it into a thin gruel, something like cornmeal mush. The tea, sugar, and milk they boiled together in large coffee tins and drank for breakfast, again at mid-morning, and at tea time in the late afternoon.

I bought their meat along with ours at a butcher shop in town. At most of the shops fresh meat and poultry lay on the counters or hung outside on hooks all day, exposed to the dust and hot sun and usually black with flies. Gloria Hagberg, bless her, steered me to a shop where the meat, though unrefrigerated, was at least displayed in glass cases protected from the flies. My weekly purchases usually included "minced beef" and maybe some steak or a "joint" for the family, as well as three-and-one-half pounds a week of "head meat" (whatever that was) for Chumley, the dog we had inherited from some departing Americans. I bought "stewing steak" for the servants, which they said they preferred. They liked their meat chewy and thought ours was "too soft." I carefully avoided the "boy meat" (for servants) that the butcher shops carried. Head meat was bad enough—often gristly and a little ripe—but the offensive boy meat, from its outrageous name to its disgusting smell, was worse.

There seemed to be no good reason why Marikus should be taking food from the unlocked store. Maybe he was sharing it with his "brothers" or friends. Maybe he was selling it. Who knew?

"Thank you, Ali," I said. "I'll speak to Marikus, but I'm not going to lock the store."

"*Hii mbaya sana.* (This is very bad.)," he said, shaking his head as he returned to his dusting. I was clearly not behaving like a proper memsahib. Because of my limited Swahili, the servants and I vastly overworked the Swahili phrases *"mbaya sana"* and *"mzuri sana"* (very bad and very good). We seldom achieved any finer distinctions in meaning. Mbaya sana could describe anything from the dog tracking mud into the hall to the death of a close relative. Facial expressions, sign language, and guesswork played as large a part in our communication as the spoken word.

That same day I had a confrontation with Marikus. "I know you've been taking tea and sugar and other things from the store, Marikus," I said. "And I want you to stop immediately."

His buck-toothed smile faded.

"I have taken nothing, madam," he said angrily, reverting to the more formal address that he had learned at school.

"Yes, well, just make sure you don't," I said.

For a few days he sulked. The brassy voice I often heard raised in arguments with the other servants was stilled, and for a while nothing was missing from the store. Then, small amounts of tea, sugar, flour and oil began once again to disappear.

What to do? Exasperating as Marikus was—and apparently a petty thief too—I was reluctant to fire him. He had a wife and would probably soon have children to support, and besides, I didn't want to have to find another "cook" and start all over again to train him. Before the Mau Mau Emergency most servants, including cooks, had been Kikuyu, but sadly, in 1957 the Kikuyu were almost all gone from Nairobi. Not one person I knew had a single Kikuyu servant. Their places had been taken by other Africans, many of whom had had little experience or training, especially cooks.

And Marikus did have some saving graces. He was eager to learn how to cook and was almost fanatically clean. He always wore a clean *kanzu*, kept the kitchen spotless, and was careful to wash his hands whenever he entered the house. So in the end, after talking it over with Bob, I decided to overlook the pilfering unless it got seriously out of hand.

The so-called locked store remained open—except when Bob and I went out at night. This had nothing to do with Marikus. I locked it to keep Cathy and Robbie from raiding the cookies, chocolate chips, and candy, ordered from the States and stored there.

One night when we were out to dinner, Cathy tried to squeeze her hand through the grille to get a candy bar. She got her hand partway in before it stuck. Twist and pull it as she might, she couldn't get it free. Robbie called Ali, who promptly doubled over with laughter at Cathy's predicament. Robbie finally got some soap and freed his sister's hand before we returned home. Bob and I heard about the incident years later. It was part of the secret life that the children and servants were beginning to share and that we usually knew nothing about.

I often felt that the servants knew everything there was to know about us, all our little habits, the family squabbles, who our friends were, where we went when we went out. But we knew about them only what they wanted us to know. Though we spent most of our waking hours together, whole chunks of their lives remained private, like another layer of living that went on somewhere out of sight, unknown and perhaps unknowable to us, so different were our lives. I was aware of the distance between us, in spite of how fond I was becoming of Ali and Rachel. Marikus was just plain incomprehensible. I never knew for sure what was going on behind that grinning, loud-voiced facade.

Marikus had gone to a mission school in Nyanza Province and had learned to speak some English, though he had difficulty reading it. When January came, he and Ali asked if they could sign up for a course in English being offered by the government at the police barracks next to Muthaiga School. Bob and I, impressed at their willingness to give up their afternoon time-off to study English, paid the small fee. For the next few months, on three afternoons a week, the two of them rode along with me when I took the children back to school after lunch and again when I picked them up. When we were out at night they would bring their English books into the living room and sit by the fire with Rachel while Cathy and Robbie helped them with their lessons.

Marikus was a quick study in the kitchen. He soon memorized the recipes for several meals and could produce them without my assistance. Prawns, however, he refused to have anything to do with. When I brought them from the market, plump and pink and flown up fresh from the Coast, he recoiled in disgust. "*Dudus* (insects), memsahib! Make you sick!"

Backing off, he put his hands behind his back, refusing to touch, let alone cook or eat such unappetizing creatures. To Ali, a cheerful young Giriama from the Coast, prawns were neither threat nor mystery. He willingly helped me clean and cook them. His energy and enthusiasm for whatever task lay at hand seemed inexhaustible. He strongly disapproved of my doing any kind of housework, except possibly cooking, and was always on the alert lest I take on chores that were his. If, from long habit, I picked up a broom after breakfast to sweep the hall, or a cloth to dust a living room table, Ali would be there before breakfast the next morning, industriously sweeping and dusting. I suggested several times that it wasn't necessary to clean every room in the house every single day. Ali would look at me as though I had uttered heresy, and go right on cleaning every room, every day. Some previous memsahib had instilled the habit and nothing I could say was going to change it

Energetic as he was, though, his devotion to his job stopped short of cleaning the four *choos* (toilets—rhymes with snows.) This seemed to be nobody's job. When I mentioned this to the servants, they were embarrassed and evasive. For whatever reason, cultural taboos or otherwise, the choos remained untouched. In the end, unhampered by taboos and armed with years of experience, I made the rounds several times weekly with my bucket and cleanser.

Ali and Marikus

7

MARKETING: FROM KARIOKOR TO KIGWARU

With supermarkets still unknown in Nairobi, Kelly and I made the rounds of a variety of small shops and markets, starting with the African market in Kariokor Location where I bought the servants their weekly bags of posho. Spread on the ground were piles of sweet potatoes, cassavas, and coconuts among stalks of bananas, a few green vegetables wilting in the sun, and the sacks of posho I had come for. But first I exchanged the customary polite greetings with the African vendor, usually a woman.

"*Jambo*, Mama!"

"*Jambo, memsahib! Habari?*" (Hello! What's the news?)

"*Mzuri sana! Habari yako?*" (Very good! What's your news?)

"*Mzuri sana! Habari mtoto?*" nodding at Kelly. (Very good! What's the news of your child?)

"*Mzuri sana!*"

And so on, until we had inquired about each other's health, homes, and husbands, and I had reached the limits of my Swahili.

Then, "*Nne, tafadhali*, four, please," I would say, pointing to the posho, and our weekly ritual was finished..

From there, Kelly and I went in and out of the row of shops in the small shopping center at Westlands, near Muthaiga: the butcher, the baker, the dairy, and Mr. Singh the greengrocer's for fruits and vegetables. At the big indoor City Market in the center of Nairobi I bought whatever produce I couldn't find at Mr. Singh's. Long rows of stands displayed great colorful mounds of oranges and pineapples, mangoes and paw paws, artichokes, avocados, peppers, tomatoes, and whole stalks of bananas, from foot-long green plantains to the tiny, delicious red finger bananas that we peeled and ate by the handful. All the familiar vegetables were there in abundance except broccoli and celery. We managed to raise several crops of broccoli in our garden, with seeds sent by my mother, but we did without celery. Two years later, sailing home to America on the USS Constitution, we astonished our waiter by devouring quantities of celery at every meal, as fast as he could refill the platter. We hadn't known till then that we had missed it so much.

Along one side of the City Market the fishmongers' wares were spread out on dripping counters: piles of huge pink prawns flanked by strange-looking, iridescent fish from the Indian Ocean, and tilapia—silvery fish from Lake Victoria, glistening in layers of ice and sawdust.

The flower stall at one end of the market drew me like a magnet. I couldn't resist the huge bunches of pink carnations, purple violets, yellow and white chrysanthemums, daisies, lilies, sweet peas and roses that filled the tiers of shelves. For three shillings, or about forty-two cents, I could bring home a multi-hued, fragrant armful.

Outdoors, in crowded stalls behind the market, African vendors sold curios: elephant hair bracelets, fly whisks, skin-covered drums, baskets, masks, wooden stools and carvings. Cathy and Robbie started collections of the carved wooden animals, bargaining enthusiastically with the vendors over prices, a game both sides seemed equally to enjoy.

When I wanted a chicken, or a turkey for Thanksgiving or Christmas, Kelly and I drove out the Limuru Road to the Kigwaru Poultry Farm. Run by a family of blond Scandinavians, the farm nestled in a hollow off the main road. Green grass, flowers, and tidy buildings surrounded a quaint farmhouse with a beautifully thatched roof. A handsome flock of half-wild crowned cranes roamed outside the barnyard, viciously attacking anything smaller than themselves. Kelly needed no persuasion to remain safely in the car.

Marikus would hang the fresh-killed turkey in the garage for a day or two to age. "Make it soft," he said. Though I worried at first that the unrefrigerated turkeys might spoil, they never did, and instead were tender and delicious. Sometimes we got our chickens alive and squawking—gifts from African friends like the Njoroges. The children made pets of them and refused to eat them, and as time went on our flock grew. I had to arrange with Ali for one to disappear now and then into the servants' cooking pots. The rest pecked their way around the back yard by day and roosted in an empty shed near the quarters where Ali shut them at night.

I always dreaded the last stop, at the Indian charcoalmaker's in a weedy field beside the road. I would park on the gravelly ground near his shack and shout down the hill to where smoke rose from the crude mounds of smoldering charcoal. "*Makaa, tafadhali!*" (Charcoal, please!)

When I finally got his attention he would bellow at his two African helpers to drag my four bags of charcoal up the hill to the car. He himself—obese, sweating, and grimy with soot—would climb the hill empty-handed behind them and smile obsequiously as I counted out the five shillings a bag. His African wife, watching from the doorway of their shack, never answered my greeting of "*Jambo.*" Always several naked children played listlessly in the dirt, staring at Kelly and me with big dark eyes.

Like the fine black charcoal dust that cast a pall over the hill, an unspoken hostility clouded the air. I was white, and compared to them I was rich, with a big car and an easy life. There was no possibility for the kind of good-natured exchange I had had with the woman in Kariokor. The family and the African helpers were sunk in a level of misery I could barely comprehend and could do nothing about. With a mixture of frustration and guilty relief I would get back in the car and drive away.

The two older children were gradually losing their yearning for hamburgers and milk shakes, and when they occasionally went to town with me after school Cathy would ask, "Mom, can we stop off at Mr. Nanji's for some curried peas?" They were rapidly becoming her favorite snack.

Taj Nanji, a tall, friendly Indian who spoke beautiful clipped English, ran the provision store across from the City Market, where I went for staples: flour, sugar, tea, oil, and packets of Cathy's curried dried peas. It took me a while to learn what to ask for. Cornstarch, for instance, was corn flour, molasses was treacle, granulated sugar was castor sugar, cookies were called biscuits, biscuits were scones. Taj patiently piloted me through the peculiarities of British English.

Taj was one of the many Indian shopkeepers in Kenya. Most were descended from Indian laborers brought to East Africa in the late 19th century to build the Uganda Railway across Kenya, connecting the coast with the shores of Lake Victoria and the lucrative markets of Uganda. The British, unable to persuade enough Africans to undertake this grueling work, had transported more than thirty thousand "coolies" from India. In her biography, *Isak Dinesen*, Judith Thurman described the horrendous task of laying the track.

"These heroic coolies," she wrote, "dragged six hundred miles of iron through malarial swamps and across deserts, throwing viaducts over ravines, climbing up escarpments and descending into torrid valleys. They also succumbed by the hundreds to fever and parasites, and to the man-eating lions."

The lions of Tsavo alone claimed the lives of twenty-eight Indian workers, an unrecorded number of Africans, and the European Superintendent of the Railway Police, who in June, 1900, was seized by a lion while sleeping in his railway carriage on a siding. He was dragged into the bush, killed, and partially eaten.

Many years later, at the East Africa Women's League farmers' market in Nairobi, I met an elderly retired railway official, a Mr. Davidson, who told me the story of the unfortunate Railway Superintendent. He said that in fact, the railway car the Superintendent was using was later Mr. Davidson's own car.

"Before it could be used again," he said, "I was told that the servants had to scrub out some terrible bloodstains."

The job of building what some called the "Lunatic Railroad" took five years. When it was completed in 1901, it shortened the trip between the coast and Nairobi from six weeks to less than twenty-four hours, and opened up the interior for trade and settlement.

Seven thousand of the Indian laborers stayed on in East Africa. They fanned out over Kenya, Tanganyika, and Uganda, becoming clerks, skilled workers, and owners of small *dukas* (shops) in every town and settlement. By 1957 about 175,000 were living in Kenya, many of them in Nairobi. One of them was our friend and Bob's tennis partner, Hassan Rattansi, who owned a sporting goods store in Nairobi. He was his own best advertisement: athletically built, good-looking, an excellent tennis player and a great cricketer. His father, he told us, had arrived in Kenya in 1899, the year the railroad reached Nairobi.

"My father told his family in India that he was only going to Bombay to look for work," Hassan said, "but his real intention was to come to East Africa. So really, he ran away. His marriage to my mother had already been arranged and the wedding had taken place, and later she joined him here in Kenya. He was unable to go to Mombasa to meet the boat, so he sent his uncle instead. Men and women didn't talk much to each other in those days. It wasn't proper. So my father's uncle waited until all the people went away and there was only himself and one woman left; then he went up to her and said, 'I am your uncle!' and brought her back to Nairobi."

Hassan's father went to work for an Indian named Visram who owned many *dukas* all over East Africa. He became manager of Visram's shop in the small upcountry town of Nyeri, where Hassan and his brothers and sisters were born, and was eventually able to buy it.

"My father was a tough man," Hassan said. "He used to walk from Nairobi to Nyeri with supplies of goods for the store in Nyeri and for trading: salt, *Amerikani* cloth, and other staples which he traded with the Africans for skins. The trip took ten days, over elephant trails and through mountains and forests. There were no roads. He and sometimes my mother walked up to Limuru, down the escarpment into the Rift Valley, then up over the Aberdares. The trip was very dangerous. There were hundreds of elephant and rhino in the forest then.

"On one of their trading trips my father and mother and my older sister, then a child of two, spent the night sleeping in a Kikuyu hut high up in the mountains. It was very cold, and when my parents woke up in the morning, my sister was dead. She had frozen to death.

"My mother was only eighteen," Hassan added.

I was haunted by the thought of the young mother, shivering with cold in the dark forest on the mountain, waking up at dawn to find her dead baby beside her—a baby the same age as Kelly was now.

Hassan's eyes were sad. Then he shrugged. Many babies died back then.

8

RANI AND MADI

Bob and I joined the United Kenya Club almost as soon as we arrived in Nairobi. Gloria and Gordon Hagberg were already members and invited us to one of the weekly Wednesday lunches, where we met the congenial mix of Asians, Africans, Americans, and English who became our friends for the next two years.

The Club had been formed in the early 1950's by a small group of people who had the radical idea that Kenya's future should be built on a multiracial society. Back then, the Club was one of the few places in East Africa where Africans, Asians, and Europeans could get together to eat and socialize in public. Almost everywhere else—restaurants, hotels, coffee shops—Kenya's own version of apartheid prevailed. Not quite as harsh as South Africa's, but close.

Many of the African and Asian friends whom we met at the Club went on after Kenya's independence to become government ministers and prominent businessmen, but when we knew them in the Fifties, they were still battling the crushing restrictions under which they lived. They were not permitted to own land in the fertile "White Highlands," were forced to live in segregated areas, and were unequally represented in the Legislative Council. In addition, Africans could not move about without observing curfews and carrying their passbooks.

Although in the United States African-Americans were never required to carry passbooks, nevertheless segregation and racial discrimination were all too common in our own not-so-distant past. Our friend Eduardo Mondlane, whom we had met in Washington, was a Mozambican who had escaped the Portuguese colonial rulers of his country. Educated in the United States, he later became the leader of Mozambique's independence movement. But when we knew him in the early 1950's, we were appalled to learn that he could not find a hotel where he could stay nor a restaurant where he could eat between Washington and New York, where he worked at the United Nations.

Still, by 1957 schools in the United States were slowly being desegregated, Congress had already passed some laws against discrimination, and we were edging toward a more equitable treatment of minorities. Being in Kenya was like taking an unfortunate step backward into our own past. The country seemed bogged down in a place that I hoped we in the United States had begun to leave behind. The existence of the United Kenya Club, as a venue for mixed-race gatherings, was one encouraging sign of progress.

Lunch at the Club was usually followed by a speaker, someone like Tom Mboya, who had organized the labor movement in Kenya despite stubborn opposition from the government and white settlers, and who was one of the first elected African members of the Legislative Council. Or pharmacist/photographer John Karmali, whose photographs of Kenya's magnificent birds and flowering plants would one day be published in two handsome books.

John once told Bob and me a story that aptly illustrated the strict segregation that dominated Kenyan life in those days. It involved one of John's early skirmishes in a stronghold of Kenya's white settlers—the Nairobi Rotary Club.

"I was the first 'brown man' to be invited to join," he said. "And soon afterward I was asked to make the 'appreciation speech' following an exhibition of paintings. I made some complimentary remarks about the paintings and the speaker, then I said, 'But isn't it a shame that the Nairobi Art Society should be For Europeans Only!'

"I sat down amidst deafening silence! They all hated me after that, but I just kept on going to their meetings anyway and spoiling their lunches." He sighed, then added, "We just had to keep push, push, pushing them all the time."

John later went on to serve in many important posts in Kenya, and became one of the country's most distinguished citizens, one who successfully bridged the gaps between Asians, Africans, and Europeans. He also eventually served as Chairman of the Nairobi Rotary Club.

Our expanding circle of friends included Madi and Rani Khurana, whom we had met at a Consulate party when we first arrived in Kenya. Their son Mahadav was about Robbie's age, and the boys frequently got together to play after school or spend the night at each other's houses. It wasn't until many years later that Robbie confessed that under his bed Mahadav kept a collection of Indian magazines displaying pictures of well-oiled, naked brown female bodies. Probably more often than Rani and I guessed, they got into mischief together—like the time they decided to trek from our house to the Khuranas' and against all orders crossed on logs over the bilharzia-infested Mathare River. They were met by a wrathful Rani, who discovered them coming up the hill behind her house. Robbie still remembers the scolding she gave them. Whatever other pranks they thought up, I don't think they tried to cross the river again.

Rani and I became part of an informal international women's group that met in each others' homes two or three mornings a month for coffee. The group included American and Indian women, a few English and other Europeans, one Japanese, and sometimes one or two African women, like Jemima Gecaga and Doctor Mwathi's wife, Jambe. It was difficult to overcome the shyness of other African women we knew and get them to come, though we tried.

The Indian women, graceful and pretty in their colorful saris, with their black hair and red caste marks on their foreheads, welcomed this opportunity to get out among other women and socialize. Some of them had to stand up to their husbands in order to attend. I remember one of them, Amrit, saying that her husband, a dentist and an educated and presumably enlightened man, objected to her going out socially without him and in fact forbade it. Amrit told him she would continue to do it just the same. Her husband was stunned speechless. "He'll just have to get used to it," Amrit said firmly.

The refreshments we served at our coffees reflected our nationalities. Sometimes we ate American banana bread and muffins, other times English biscuits and scones, or spicy Indian *samosas* and honeyed fried dough. Interest in food was a common bond, and we began to include cooking as part of our get-togethers. Rani demonstrated how to make curry, I made lemon meringue pie, and the Japanese Consul General's wife stood over a charcoal brazier on her dining room table and stir-fried heaps of mysterious Japanese ingredients in a cast iron *sukiaki* pan. The names of many of the women I cooked and ate with live on in my recipe file. When I take out the cards, memories come flooding back of a roomful of dark and light faces, of fluttering saris, of laughter and chatter in a medley of accents, and of the fiery taste of one of Rani's curries.

When we were invited to the Khuranas for dinner, we never knew what to expect—Indian curry, Chinese stir-fry, or an Indonesian feast of *satay* with *gadoh-gadoh* sauce and rice cooked in coconut milk. Though Rani was a Moslem and Madi a Hindu, nevertheless crispy bits of pork and, I suspected, sometimes beef—the first forbidden to Moslems, the second to Hindus—often found their way into Rani's Chinese and Malaysian dishes. I don't think either Rani or Madi ever let religious taboos get in their way. Rani told me once that both their families had opposed their marriage.

"We had to turn Sikh to get married," she said. "It was the only way!"

Madi was a career diplomat with the Indian High Commission (embassy) who later became an ambassador. He was invariably proper and polite, careful to observe all the niceties of diplomatic protocol, but I could often detect a twinkle of amusement in his eye. I loved to watch him and Rani play tennis, Rani in loose cotton trousers and tunic, bouncing around on the court like a beautiful escapee from a Malaysian rice paddy, and Madi, in immaculate white shorts and shirt and with an impeccable British accent, calling encouragingly across the net, "Good shot, Mama. Veddy nice!"

Rani was from Singapore, the daughter of Malaysian and Chinese parents. Almond eyes and high cheekbones in the smooth ivory oval of her face revealed her Chinese heritage. She drew her black hair straight back into a shining bun, worn low on her plump neck. Into it she often tucked a fresh white gardenia or a crimson hibiscus.

One day when I was there for coffee, she showed me the dozens of exquisite saris that filled her closet: black silks embroidered in silver or gold, filmy flowered prints in delicate lavenders and pinks, electric blue chiffons, vivid turquoises, intricately patterned scarlets, yellows and golds. She wore them gracefully, draping the soft folds on a generous but shapely figure.

I knew that Rani and Madi had met during World War II in Singapore, where Madi was stationed with the British Army, but years later their son Mahadav told me more of their story. Toward the end of the war, he said, his father had joined a number of Indian troops who broke away from the British and fought for Indian independence. Later Madi was honored as a hero and awarded a medal by the Indian government, but meanwhile the British arrested him and threw him into jail in India.

As soon as the war was over Rani, back in Singapore, somehow got herself onto a troopship—the only woman among 2000 men—and went to India to look for Madi.

"And found him!" said Mahadav. "She's a strong woman, my mother!"

When I heard this story, I had a hard time picturing the suave diplomat I knew as a revolutionary soldier, but I had no trouble at all imagining Rani on a troopship, holding her own among two thousand soldiers.

Madi retired after a distinguished career in India's diplomatic service, and he and Rani live in New Delhi now. He recently wrote that they have given up tennis for the less strenuous game of golf. Even so, he said, "We only play once a week. The rest of the time, we rest!"

I could picture that same old gleam of amusement in his eyes as he wrote this oblique reference to our aging selves.

Frank LaMacchia from the U.S. Consulate with Kelly, me, Madi and Rani
Khurana, and Lillian LaMacchia on a Sunday afternoon in Kiambu

9

A FAREWELL PARTY, FLYING ANTS, AND THE RESURRECTION OF PETRO'S MOTHER

The long rains began in late March 1958, with a few hard showers, mostly at night. A distinct weather change accompanied them: cloudy days when the wind was damp and cool—the monsoon wind, blowing in from the coast. It reminded me of early fall in New England with a northeaster brewing.

Along with the rains, our belongings finally arrived in two packing crates, after being traced to the Baltimore wharf where they had been lying forgotten. It was like a delayed Christmas when we began unpacking. First out were some treats we never found in Nairobi: American cake mixes and chocolate chips, cans of Hershey's syrup (a popular hostess gift to friends in Nairobi), and packages of popcorn. We lined them up in the "locked store" and gloated over the beautiful American labels. For the next few days we gorged ourselves on brownies and chocolate chip cookies and popcorn. The children had a popcorn party after school for a gang of their friends, and invited the servants too. Ali and Marikus thought we were performing some kind of magic when fluffy white morsels began exploding from the hard yellow kernels.

While the children pulled from the boxes familiar dolls and books and toys, Bob and I unpacked our own books, our stereo and records, our favorite chairs, and hung our own pictures on the walls. I discovered that five jars of my mother's homemade beach plum jelly, mistakenly included by the packers, had miraculously survived the trip. With our own things around us, and with my mother's jelly on our breakfast toast, we finally felt at home.

As soon as we had unpacked and gotten settled, we were ready to give our first official reception. Ninety people were invited to wish farewell to Samson

Mwathi, who was leaving for a tour of the United States. He would be traveling on a Leader Grant awarded by our government to prominent citizens of other countries, for which Bob and Gordon had nominated him. Educated at Makerere College in Uganda, Samson Mwathi was among the first African doctors in Kenya, and also one of the first persons from his country to receive a Leader Grant. There were few Africans then in any of the professions, and those few were respected and admired by other Africans. As a result, leadership roles were often thrust upon them. The Leader Grants provided an opportunity for them to broaden their horizons and learn more about the modern technological world, meet colleagues who could help them become conversant with developments in their own fields, and gain an understanding of Americans and American culture. When he returned three months later, Dr. Mwathi would tell us with great enthusiasm that "everyone was marvelous" to him. He had received the rare honor of becoming a fellow of the American College of Physicians and Surgeons and had made many friends. Like that of other Leader Grantees during those years, Dr. Mwathi's experience was evidence that this kind of program worked. It was one of our government's more successful efforts abroad and created a corps of people from other countries who remained America's friends.

The farewell party provided us with an opportunity to meet more local people, and with Dr. Mwathi's help we added many of his African friends to the invitation list along with Asians, Americans, and other Europeans. Entertaining on such a scale was a new experience for me. At home when we had friends or neighbors over for dinner, we invited perhaps three other couples at most and it was usually potluck, with everyone bringing part of the meal. So it was with some trepidation that I tackled the planning of a party of this magnitude. In the end I did it the way I do most things—by making lists, and then more lists. I multiplied all the ingredients I would need by ten, and hoped for the best.

It took the better part of four days, once I had my lists in hand, to get ready for the party: shopping for food and with Marikus's help preparing it, arranging flowers, borrowing ten dozen glasses and a huge punch bowl from USIS.

One thing I never had to worry about back home was having titled neighbors drop in. Not so in Kenya. The afternoon before the big event I was in the kitchen chopping garlic for one of the dips when the doorbell rang. The servants were having their time off, so I gave my hands a quick wipe on my apron and answered the door myself. Baron von Stackleburg, the German Consul General, stood on the front step—blond, erect, clicking his heels and bowing. He and his wife had recently rented the house next door. Their little daughter attended Muthaiga

School and we sometimes car-pooled the children. He had come this afternoon to arrange a ride for Marina.

Before I knew what was happening, he was taking my hand and kissing it—the same hand that only a moment ago had been clutching raw garlic. I repressed the impulse to snatch my hand away and stood there, helpless and embarrassed. Baron von Stackleburg gallantly concealed the olfactory shock he must have received, but left quickly after I agreed to pick up Marina at school. The next time he came to the house he was as correct and courteous as ever, but he omitted the hand kissing. I can't say I blamed him.

On the night of the party, two *askaris* remained on duty outside the house all evening, directing traffic and helping guests park. Such large, racially mixed gatherings were rare in Muthaiga, but because it was an "official" function for a widely respected grantee, there were no overt objections from either government or neighbors—at least as far as we knew.

The Hagbergs brought along their houseboy, Zabulon, to help Ali serve. Marikus was busy in the kitchen, refilling trays of canapes and keeping the cheese sticks and tiny meatballs hot. In the living room we opened the French doors to the garden. The rain held off; the night was lovely. Floodlights illuminated a scene like a stage set: Indian ladies with shining dark hair and brilliant saris, African faces above gleaming white shirt collars, the pale blur of Europeans in evening dress. The white-robed figures of Ali and Zabulon edged through the crowd, holding high their loaded trays. The lights glinted on their gold embroidered scarlet vests, and their red fezzes appeared and reappeared like bright buoys on the sea of people.

Magenta and orange bougainvillea, red hibiscus, and smooth green lawn formed the backdrop. Beyond the flowers and grass, out where the floodlights couldn't reach, the forest was a dense, invisible presence held at bay by the lights, the color, the noise, the people.

The children sat in their pajamas on the stair landing, Kelly in the middle flanked protectively by Cathy and Robbie, and watched all evening. From their vantage point they beckoned to Ali every time he passed below with a tray of food, and held court with the many people who spotted them and climbed the stairs for a chat.

The invitations had read Reception 5:00-8:00 P.M., but by now I had been to enough cocktail parties and receptions in Kenya to expect what would happen. I planned a buffet substantial enough to count as dinner: meatballs, *samosas*, cassava chips and dips, crackers and cheeses, platters of cold meats and raw vegetables, rolls, and brownies and an assortment of fruits for dessert. And sure enough, the party went on full blast until after eleven, when the guests began to depart. Dr. Mwathi stood with us at the door, pumping hands with departing guests, his wide-spaced teeth protruding in a happy smile as he accepted good wishes for his trip.

The house was a shambles, but with help from Ali and Marikus, Bob and I soon had it cleaned up. It was one of the many times I was thankful the servants were there after all. After everyone else had gone to bed, I stood looking out at a garden and forest softened by a sheen of moonlight, remembering my fears about coming here. Violence might lie just under the surface, but Kenya was a place I was coming to love.

The long rains also brought the after-rain flight of the flying ants. New to this phenomenon, I neglected to close all the windows, and after the first hard shower droves of insects emerged from the ground and filled the air. Transparent wings vibrating, they flew in all directions and in through the open windows. Bodies and wings littered the floors throughout the house. Ali swept up great mounds of them in every room. Outside, the other servants were eagerly gathering them up to be eaten as a tasty snack. Kelly must have been watching, because we discovered her later in the dining room, crunching happily on a few brittle bodies that Ali had missed. Cathy and Robbie reacted with a horrified "Yuck!" Bob and I looked at each other and tried not to laugh.

"How about a peanut butter and jelly sandwich instead?" I asked. Kelly swallowed and nodded her head.

The rains were the time for planting, and after seeing Rani's spectacular garden, I asked if she would help me rescue ours. It had become wild and jungly under Petro, the gardener's, indifferent care. He diligently hosed down the car every morning, scraped the mud from our shoes and polished them to a high shine, but gardening was clearly not high on his list of priorities. I constantly prodded him to take his *panga* and prune the never-ending explosion of growth that was overwhelming the garden. In a climate that combined the warmth of the equatorial sun with cool nights and bountiful rains, flowers and shrubs seemed to burst from the soil vibrating with color and energy. I gloried in the scarlet hibiscus blanketing the huge bushes, in the blaze of bougainvillea that cascaded from the treetops. When we went home two years later to the gritty grayness of Washington in January, I ached for the greenness and flowers of Kenya.

But constant weeding and pruning were essential to keep the garden from swallowing the house, and Petro was not eager to do either. He seldom spoke or smiled and seemed to live in a silent world that was hard to penetrate. I would greet him in the morning with a "*Jambo, habari?*" (Hello, how are you?) and he would grunt a barely audible "*Jambo.*" I could never figure out whether he was just shy, or had a grudge against women who wanted him to weed and prune.

When Rani and I appeared with our baskets of cuttings and plants that we had dug from her flourishing flower beds for transplanting to mine, Petro visibly wilted, then vanished at the first opportunity. With and without his help, we transformed the bed along the front of the house into a colorful riot of flowers. Under the dining room windows, there was already a magical bush called Yesterday, Today, and Tomorrow. With a kind of horticultural sleight-of-hand, it produced sweet-smelling blossoms of purple, lavender, and white, all at the same time.

We spent days making a border of pink ivy geranium along the stone wall around the side lawn, and where the forest began we set some tall cannas. They grew to six feet in no time, with bronzy leaves and huge orange and crimson flowers that waved like brilliant pennants from the far end of the garden.

One day a wire came to Bob's office saying that Petro's mother had died. With Ali as interpreter, Bob told him the sad news and gave him a month's leave to go home. After several weeks he returned, but a short time later he requested, through Ali, permission to go home again. It seemed a letter had come saying his "Mama *kufa*"—his mother had died. Again?

"But he went home last time because his mother had died," I protested to Ali.

Big smile. "*Ndio*, memsahib. But then his mother resumed life, and now, again, she is dead."

I never really knew what happened to Petro's mother. Had she just been ill or in a coma the first time, and recovered? Had I misunderstood what Ali had said? Was this just an excuse to go on leave again? My Swahili was not up to framing the right questions and Ali's English was inadequate for furnishing answers. The deaths and resurrection of Petro's mother remain forever one of Africa's mysteries.

When Petro returned weeks later from his second trip home, he seemed less interested in gardening than ever. Reluctantly, we finally had to let him go. When Ali told him, he accepted the news and departed, phlegmatic as ever. Ali found us another gardener, a spindly old man named Mukolwe who had a gentle smile and a passion for growing things. For the rest of the time we were in Kenya, he puttered happily in the garden, diligently weeding and pruning and watering, tending the flowers and shrubs with utter devotion.

10

SUNDAY SAFARIS AND WILD BEES

Safari is the Swahili word for journey—any kind of journey, long or short. We began taking the children on "Sunday safaris," picking a different road out of Nairobi each time and following it into the countryside. Sometimes we went to the Ngong Hills and picnicked above the tree line in high green meadows full of wild flowers, where the wind sang through the long grasses. Beyond the Hills, to the west, stretched mile after empty mile of the vast Rift Valley, a gigantic fault in the earth's surface so deep and wide it can be seen from space. It cracks open the planet's crust from the Red Sea down through the heart of the African continent to what was then called Nyasaland and is now Malawi. From the top of the hills we could sometimes see, far down on the valley floor, a lone giraffe or a pair of zebras, like miniatures from a child's toy zoo.

South of the hills lay Olorgesailie, a prehistoric site where Louis and Mary Leakey had uncovered one of the world's richest deposits of stone axes and scrapers and bones. For more than half a century the Leakeys and their sons dug in dusty layers of primordial African earth, searching East Africa for fossil records of early man. They found skulls and bone fragments of some of our early ancestors, who inhabited East Africa millions of years ago. Mary Leakey's discovery in 1976 of three sets of footprints leading across a plain in northern Tanzania took the record back three-and-three-quarter million years, when three hominids—probably two adults and a child—walked upright across an expanse of damp volcanic ash. It hardened and captured for all time a haunting record of a moment in their existence. Theirs are perhaps some of our earliest ancestors' footprints.

When I first landed in Kenya, I gave little thought to the fact that I was stepping onto a part of the earth where the first humans had walked. But visiting Olorgasailie shone an illuminating light into that distant past and evoked a sharp sense of the antiquity of this African land.

In blistering heat one Sunday, with Kelly in her sunbonnet clinging to my hand, we walked the narrow catwalks that threaded the dig. On these parched acres of desert-like terrain, under a brutally hot sun, the Leakeys and their African assistants had patiently swept and sifted the dry earth. The ancient relics they found were meticulously laid out in labeled rows surrounded by earthen dikes topped by the catwalks—an outdoor archeological museum as well as a working dig.

Dazzled by the sun, I imagined the shadows of early people hovering over this site, once a tree-fringed lake. Human hands had fashioned these tools. Real men and women had hunted and eaten the animals whose flesh once covered these bones. Here they had lived, worked, killed, been born and perhaps died. I could almost feel their presence. Cathy and Robbie stood beside me, wide-eyed and silent, as though they too sensed something otherworldly about the site.

We ate our lunch at a picnic table, sheltered under a thatched roof from the unrelenting sun. The European warden and African guide who supervised the site told us it became so cold at night, once the sun had gone, that they had to sleep under blankets. Perhaps the climate had changed since prehistoric times; if not, the early people who had lived beside this vanished lake would surely have needed the furs of those animals they had killed, to keep them warm at night.

Sometimes these Sunday safaris took us nowhere and when we arrived we wondered why we had come. Lake Magadi was as godforsaken a spot as you could find anywhere on earth, as we discovered when we yielded to an impulse. On the way back from Olorgesailie to the main road, we noticed a gravelly track that crawled away haphazardly through sparse bush.

"Lake Magadi," read a sign nailed to a spindly tree. An arrow pointed south. It was early afternoon; we had plenty of time before dark. Lake Magadi looked invitingly blue and cool on the map. So…why not?

The monotony of the thirty-mile drive through a thin cover of yellow-green fever trees was relieved only when we sighted game: an unusually large herd of giraffe—we counted forty-eight—that stood frozen in the hot stillness, blinking at us from the middle of the road. We were almost upon them before they broke and galloped away, dissolving like a mirage in the heat haze. Or three dainty dik diks kicking up their tiny heels as they dashed into the bush, and occasionally a few gazelles or a family of baboons.

The lake, when we reached it, lay blazing white, impaled by the sun: a soda lake bordered by huge flat pans where evaporating water left behind thick deposits of ashy white soda and salt. A factory, incongruous in this remote spot, sat silent and lifeless beside the lake—closed on Sunday.

We saw not a soul, heard not a sound, just turned the car around and headed back toward Nairobi.

On another Sunday we had a frightening encounter with one of Africa's most vicious wild animals. We had been invited to accompany an archeologist friend on a small "dig" in the Rift Valley—a day's outing only. Taking our picnic lunches, our water jugs, and our children, we made up a caravan of three cars and headed out of town on the road to Naivasha.

Our archeologist was Peter Cooke, the English wife of an American in our Consulate and the mother of two little boys. Peter worked for Dr. Leakey at the Coryndon Museum in Nairobi. She was interestingly eccentric, from her name and her job to the green stockings she wore at parties and the thin cigars she smoked.

Under Peter's direction the half-dozen children in our party and an equal number of adults fanned out along an embankment a short distance off the road. Poking and prodding among the rocks, we gently brushed away the powdery clay soil, searching for stone tools or fossils. The site was not far from an area where the Leakeys had unearthed many such finds.

Without warning Robbie was screaming and running toward me over the rough hillocks of weeds, stumbling and crying and pursued by a horde of wild bees. As he reached me, the bees attacked me too.

"Stand perfectly still," Peter cautioned from nearby. But the bees were aroused and angry. They were soon furiously stinging all three of us.

African bees are small but vicious. There are stories of them attacking people alone in the bush and stinging them to death. A legendary Kenya settler, Colonel Ewart Grogan, who in his eighties was still a member of Kenya's Legislative Council during our time there, was said to have had a famous encounter with African bees. The story went that in the early 1900's, in an attempt to impress the father of his ladylove and win her hand in marriage, he walked the five thousand miles from the Cape of Good Hope to Cairo. His journey took him through remote areas of bush and forest, and in one of these he was attacked by bees.

Stripping off his bee-infested clothes as he ran, he burst, naked and pale-skinned, into an African village and dove headfirst through the doorway of a smoke-filled hut. The bees were turned back by the smoke, Colonel Grogan was saved, and the African woman in the hut had her first sight of a white man— and probably the shock of her life.

On the day we were attacked, there was no smoke-filled sanctuary, only our cars one hundred yards away. Standing still wasn't helping, and the pain from the stings was excruciating. Peter and Robbie and I began to run toward the cars. The others, still at a safe distance, thought we had gone mad. When they realized what was happening, they grabbed the remaining children and, circling us widely, also ran for the cars. Robbie and I piled in, the bees buzzing and stinging our scalps and necks. I seized our big water container and emptied it over our heads. The burning needles of pain began to ease a little.

Meanwhile Bob threw himself into the car along with Cathy and Kelly and started the engine. With the windows rolled down and bees streaming away on the wind, we raced along the road until finally the bees were left behind. Peter, whose husband had driven her at top speed to Naivasha, the nearest town, required medical treatment and was hospitalized overnight. The bees had become entangled in her long dark hair and she had over one hundred stings on her head. Bob pulled fifty-five stingers out of my head and neck, and ten from Robbie's.

For a day or two Robbie and I were achey and nauseated, the bites painful and itchy. Cathy was having nightmares about bees, more upset at witnessing what they had done to her brother and me than at the one or two stings she herself had received. By the third day Robbie and I felt better, with only minor itching, but five days later we both woke up in the night, itching all over again, worse than ever. By morning we had huge red hives on our arms and necks, and Robbie had enlarged glands and a swollen hand. Dr. Davies, our English pediatrician, prescribed some medication and ordered complete rest for both of us until all swelling and hives were gone. She said we were incredibly lucky that we weren't seriously ill and considered it a minor miracle that Peter and I were not hospitalized for several weeks. Ten days later I was still itching, though gradually improving. I didn't realize at the time how close we had come to catastrophe, but I have since read that one hundred stings by wild African bees can kill an adult.

We had one further experience with bees—not an attack, but a test of wills: ours and the bees.' Unbeknownst to us a swarm had infiltrated the space between the roof and ceiling over Kelly's bedroom. The great weight of the hive they built, filled with many pounds of honey, finally caused it to break through the ceiling. Bees came flying through the opening, buzzing confusedly about the room while honey began to drip slowly onto the floor.

There was nothing to do but move Kelly in with Cathy and close up her room. First we tried spraying. Dead bees littered the floor when we looked in later, but others still poured through the opening in the ceiling. We had hoped the survivors would leave the way they had originally come and build a new hive elsewhere, but we had reckoned without the determination of a colony of bees. This was where they would have their hive, or die in the attempt.

We next tried a series of poison smoke bombs. After each one we opened the door to see dead bees everywhere. But still the air hummed, and still the living bees crawled through the opening and zoomed into the room. It wasn't until every bee was dead, many days later, that we were able to begin the massive clean-up of dead bees and honey.

Mukolwe, our old gardener who had replaced Petro, stood on a kitchen chair and with his hands dug out the chunks of honeycomb. Honey cascaded down his head and arms, carrying with it the bodies of more dead bees. The servants were eager to eat the honey but we were afraid it had been contaminated by the poisonous smoke. Reluctantly we threw it all away.

The hole in the ceiling was patched and Kelly moved back into her room, but for a long time afterward, years even, whenever I heard the low buzzing of even one bee, I would duck for cover. When we occasionally met up with other swarms out in the African bush, I would feel a few moments of panic and look quickly for shelter, but we were never attacked again. And we continued to go on our Sunday—or longer—safaris.

11

YOUNG KENYA LEADERS AND THEIR WIVES

One morning I dropped by to see Ernestine Kiano, who was expecting a baby at any moment. She was an African American nurse from California who had married Gikonyo Kiano, a Kenyan graduate student at the University of California in Berkeley. They had returned to Kenya just the year before we arrived there ourselves.

I found Ernestine home alone, in an advanced stage of labor, clutching her belly and groaning. When she hadn't been able to reach Gikonyo, she had called a taxi. It arrived just after I did, and between us the driver and I half-carried Ernestine down the stairs and into the taxi. I stayed at the hospital the short time until the baby was safely delivered and Ernestine was sleeping, then went home and called Bob at the office. If you see Gikonyo, I said, you can tell him he's the father of a baby boy. As it happened, Gikonyo did come by the office later in the morning and got the news from Bob. The incident led to some jokes about the kind of information service the USIS was running.

Gikonyo had majored in political science at Berkeley, and had the distinction of being the first African from Kenya to receive a PhD. We heard later from his University of California advisor that he was the "brightest foreign student I ever had." Back in Kenya, he had secured a post as a lecturer in political science at the Royal Technical College—the first African on the faculty there. He and Ernestine lived in a staff flat near the College—housing for Europeans only. But as an uncle of Gikonyo's told us, laughing heartily,

"Gikonyo didn't care. He just moved in anyway!"

Bob had met Gikonyo briefly at an American Political Science Association meeting in the States, and got in touch with him soon after our arrival in Kenya. He and Ernestine often came to have dinner with us, sometimes with their son Gaylord, who was Robbie's age. I came to know Ernestine as an outspoken, determined woman who took no nonsense from anyone. Tall, heavy-browed, sometimes fierce

76

in her approach to people and problems, she chafed at the political and social restrictions under which they lived. She also complained bitterly about their low economic status and resented the drain placed on their meager resources by the demands of Gikonyo's extended family and clan, who by tribal custom expected to share in the good fortune that he supposedly enjoyed as a result of his education.

"They just keep coming down from Fort Hall and moving in," Ernestine stormed to me once. "And Gikonyo refuses to send them home!"

This was after they had moved out of the small University staff flat and into a nondescript house in a sort of no man's land between Asian, African, and European areas of Nairobi. The house was scantily furnished and poorly equipped, with a primitive kitchen and a rudimentary stove with no oven. Occasionally Ernestine tried to give dinner parties for some of the people who had entertained them since their return to Kenya, but she was fighting against difficult odds. A few times I helped by picking up roasts or casseroles from her, cooking them in my oven, then taking them back with me to the party.

On nights when Ernestine and Gikonyo came to dinner at our house, Ernestine would sit leafing through our Sears catalog, peering through her glasses and yearning for everything from clothes to couches and washing machines. One night she got carried away by pictures of a fireplace set of handsome andirons, and began fantasizing about saving enough money to send for them.

"But Ernestine," I protested. "You don't even have a fireplace!"

"I know," she sighed, and closed the catalog.

I wondered if the impractical brass andirons represented for her the familiar comfort of the home she had had back in the States, or the one she had expected to have, complete with a living room and a cozy fireplace. Bob and I did loan her money a time or two to send for a dress from the catalog. In fact, Jemima Gecaga and Dr. Mwathi's wife Jambe asked if they could order clothes from it too. There was virtually no place in Nairobi to buy women's clothing, except for cotton housedresses in the Bazaar Street dukas or Italian designer outfits in boutiques near the New Stanley Hotel. To Ernestine and Jemima and Jambe the new styles and low prices in the Sears catalog sang a siren song, and they placed their orders along with mine.

Ernestine, and other Americans married to African men, were caught in a culture clash that sometimes brought enormous pressures to bear on their marriages. The men, so well educated, seemingly so Westernized in the States, found their tribal traditions and customs, deeply ingrained since childhood, surfacing again once they were back in Kenya. The tribesman was not far beneath the skin of these apparently worldly men. Along with the clan expectation of "sharing the wealth," one of the most difficult things for American women to accept was the attitude of the men they had married toward sexual freedom. Polygamy had a long history in African cultures, and once back home, many of the men, though professed Christians, reverted to ancient custom and took second wives or mistresses. It was often the last straw for the American wives, the final intolerable act that ended the marriages.

But, ironically, to the men's own African people it was their very veneer of Westernization, the education and university degrees, that set them above the crowd, that caused them to be revered, listened to, and followed. It must have been as hard for them as it was for their wives to live with this dichotomy. They were pulled back toward the familiar tribal past and at the same time propelled forward by their education and western acculturation into the exhilarating, confusing, perhaps perilous future of modern Kenya.

Gikonyo had grown up sixty miles from Nairobi, in a part of Kikuyuland then called Fort Hall and now known as Murang'a. He first attended the village primary school near his home, then for the next two grades another school farther away.

"Those were the worst years of my life!" he told us. "1937 and 1938, walking barefoot six miles every day up and down the ridges to get to that school and back home. At the time I didn't know I was suffering, though." He laughed. "I didn't know any better!"

Even before he started school he had learned to wear clothes instead of his stiff little goatskin cloak, thanks to an older brother who gave him his shirt.

"It was very big and hung down very long, so it didn't matter that I didn't have any pants. It was a great improvement on the cloak." He laughed again. "Those skin cloaks were really just symbolic clothes, you know. They didn't cover very much!"

His next school was even farther away. Again he had to walk.

"When I went to start my first term at Nyeri," he said, "I walked all day along goat paths to get there. There were no roads. I want you to imagine this: a thirteen-year-old boy, weighing fifty-six pounds, and carrying a small bundle of books, walking all day across the hills. If I had ten cents in my pocket I might stop somewhere to buy a cup of tea or some milk. I did this at the beginning and end of each term."

He went on to graduate from Alliance High School, one of the fortunate few African boys to win a coveted place there, then to college in the States on a scholarship, and eventually to graduate school at Berkeley.

Small and slight, with thick spectacles that dominated his narrow intelligent face, Gikonyo was interested in politics from the moment he arrived back in Kenya. Because of his education he was widely respected among Africans, and very shortly was being looked on as an important young leader of his people, especially the Kikuyu. He had been in the States throughout the years of the Emergency, and so had been somewhat insulated from the trauma of Mau Mau. Acutely aware of the urgent need for higher education for Kenyans—in 1956 there were less than half a dozen high schools for five million Africans, and at most a few dozen African students attending colleges in East Africa or overseas—he began immediately to look for the means to send students to universities in the United States.

He was joined in this effort by Tom Mboya, whom we had met at the first reception we attended at the American Consul General's residence. Tom was a Luo, very dark, with high cheekbones in a round face and a kind of Cheshire cat smile. As General Secretary of the Kenya Federation of Labor, he was already well-known throughout Kenya and one of the few from his tribe who was on good terms with the Kikuyu political leaders. He had also, a few months before, been elected to the Legislative Council in the first general election in which Africans had the right to vote.

Tom had been born on a sisal farm in the "White Highlands" near Thika and attended schools in Kikuyu, Wakamba, and Luo areas, forging ties with tribes other than his own and thus growing up less "tribalized" than many Africans. During the 1950's, at the invitation of American labor leaders, he traveled several times to the United States. He was interviewed on Meet the Press, appeared on the Today show where we had seen him, and on a later trip had what he described as a very cordial meeting with Vice President Nixon.

"We talked so long, I was late for an appearance at Howard University," Tom told us when he returned home. "The Vice President insisted on driving me there himself and accompanied me into the auditorium to apologize for making me late!"

Nevertheless, despite the high-level meetings in the States, the appearances on TV, an honorary degree from Howard University, and his seat in the Legislative Council, when Tom returned to Kenya it was to a home in the African Location where he was required to live. His tiny two-room dwelling was lighted by kerosene lanterns, had a dirt floor, no bathroom, and a rude kitchen where water had to be carried from an outdoor tap. Undaunted, he, along with Gikonyo, continued his efforts to find educational opportunities for Africans.

Bob, as Cultural Affairs Officer, was deeply involved in these efforts. Increasing numbers of students began coming to him through Tom and Gikonyo, or on their own. Each morning, when he arrived at his office, he found a long line of eager young Kenyans waiting outside his door. He advised them about the choice of a college and sources of scholarship money, assisted them in filling out applications, arranged for tutoring in English, and administered the required English language exams.

Sometimes he and Gikonyo held "cultural orientation sessions" for departing students, preparing them for the cultural shock that lay ahead: the different customs, the need for warm clothing in cold climates, the importance of personal hygiene.

Gikonyo was a stern mentor about hygiene. "People in the United States have lots of water," he told them, stabbing the air with his finger to emphasize each point. "And they have lots of soap. And they use them! And they expect you to use them too! They also have more than one pair of socks and they change them every day. They expect you to do the same."

Some evenings, while I provided coffee and sandwiches, Gikonyo and Tom sat in our living room with Bob, poring over lists—lists of prospective students, lists of colleges, lists of potential donors of money. Sometimes the talk veered to politics, and Tom and Gikonyo speculated about when they might hope to achieve independence from Britain.

"Maybe in ten years, if we're lucky," Tom said.

They had no idea, nor did we, that independence was in fact only four years away. Kenya was riding on the crest of a wave of change that was sweeping with increasing rapidity over Africa. Ghana had already gained its independence in 1957, followed by Guinea a year later. Tanganyika and Uganda would be independent by 1961 and 1962 respectively, then Kenya in 1963. Tom and Gikonyo's dream was much closer to fulfillment than any of us thought.

One night I saw Tom doodling on a piece of paper, experimenting with different patterns of lines and stripes.

"I'm designing the new flag for Kenya," he said, looking up with a smile. "Black for the people and green for the land."

Sometimes he and Gikonyo seemed like little boys, playing a game.

"And red for the blood we have spilled!" added Gikonyo, and Tom's smile disappeared. It was no game after all.

As a result of all the list-making, planning, and fund-raising efforts by these men and others, planeloads of students began leaving for the United States aboard chartered flights that became known as the "Airlifts." They were paid for by contributions from private individuals in the United States, many of whom were friends and acquaintances of Tom's. A few of the students were recipients of official U.S. government scholarships that covered tuition, room, and board, but many had to raise the money themselves for their first year's expenses—astronomical sums for most. So strong was the hunger and reverence for education that to help their sons, and occasionally daughters, fathers sold precious land or went deeply into debt. One student told Bob that his father had ridden his bicycle from village to village for months until he had collected enough money for his son to go to college. Sometimes a whole village held benefit tea parties until it raised enough money to send one student to America.

In 1958, a few months after we arrived, Kariuki Njiiri and his American wife Ruth returned to Kenya with their small son, Kari. They often came to dinner with the Kianos, Tom, and others. Ruth invariably arrived promptly but usually alone. Kariuki had a cheerful disregard for time and was almost always late. He would come bursting in, sometimes an hour or more after dinner had been served, his broad brown face alight with a happy smile.

"Am I late? Sorry!" he would say, grabbing me in a bear hug.

It was hard to stay annoyed with him, especially since he was so frequently the life of the party with his high spirits and good-natured banter. After dinner he loved to roll back the rug in the living room and dance. With the record player blaring, he would fling himself out onto the floor, jitterbugging his way through a succession of partners and leaving us all exhausted.

Kariuki had grown up in a Kikuyu village, the son of Senior Chief Njiiri. As a teenager he may have heard whispers about the secret organization called Mau Mau, but before actual violence broke out his father sent him to India to attend high school, and from there to the United States. He graduated from Lincoln University and the New School of Social Research in New York, where he met Ruth.

For Ruth, who had grown up in a middle class African-American family in Massachusetts, the outright segregation of races in Kenya was a shock. She told me that back home she had always had to steel herself against the possibility of discrimination, the chance that the hotel clerk would refuse to give her a room, or the waiter in the restaurant would refuse to serve her. But most of the time it didn't happen. Here in Kenya, however, where segregated housing was imposed by law and Africans were banned from hotels and restaurants, neither Ruth nor Ernestine could live in Muthaiga, stay at the Norfolk, or meet me for lunch at the New Stanley. Ruth's good-humored acceptance of the situation masked a quiet determination to help change it.

Ruth and Kariuki joined Gikonyo Kiano and Tom Mboya in their campaign to send as many African students as possible to the United States. All of them were passionate about this mission. They saw education as their only hope of eventually freeing themselves from British domination. Independence was a far-off goal, somewhere down the road in the future. The need for education was now, and they tapped every resource they could find.

Ruth propped her typewriter on a carton in the dingy three-room flat where she and Kariuki first lived, and with Kari playing on the floor beside her, she wrote letters home to find colleges and high schools willing to accept foreign students, and to enlist scholarship aid from American friends and relatives.

Kariuki found a job as an Adult Literacy officer. In his Land Rover he traveled to outlying villages where he supervised the teaching of reading and writing to illiterate tribesmen and tribeswomen. Wherever he went, he kept his eyes open for promising students and sent them to Bob or Gikonyo or Tom.

Over the next few years, thousands of Kenyan students would be educated abroad in the United States and Canada. They would return home in the 1960's to fill some of the many vacancies in the government, professions, businesses, and industries of a newly independent Kenya. Without them the country would have been hard put to staff its new government and fill these important posts.

Tom Mboya in Luo hat and robe

12

THE DIPLOMATIC LIFE: DISTINGUISHED VISITORS, A REBELLIOUS TEEN, AND A WILD MONKEY

In a small post like Nairobi in the 1950's, we all helped entertain visiting Americans. Bob and I were hosts to many people whom we would otherwise never have known, from sports figures and journalists to senators and college presidents. One of our visitors was Chuck Coker, the track coach for Occidental College in California, who stayed with us for several weeks while he coached teams of Kenyan athletes. A Greek god of a man, he looked like a blond ad for any kind of sports equipment anyone might want to sell. He was also a health nut. Each morning we watched, mesmerized, while he downed nine different vitamin pills with his orange juice. Almost immediately he had Robbie exercising with a jump rope and me taking some of his vitamin pills for a skin condition I had developed as a result of too much equatorial sun.

Another time the Westminster Choir came from Princeton to give a series of concerts—a friendly, genial bunch of people who were excellent cultural ambassadors. The chancellor of the University of California, Clark Kerr, had dinner with us, and several senators, including Senator Dodd from Connecticut, passed through on tours of Africa.

One of our most memorable guests was Father Theodore Hesburgh, President of Notre Dame University. Bob met him when he came to Nairobi in 1958 on a tour of Africa and was so charmed by his enthusiasm and friendliness that he invited him home to dinner. I was expecting a white-haired, saintly character, but Father Hesburgh was anything but that. Tall, handsome, with heavy black brows and close-cropped dark hair, he was full of youthful energy and high spirits, and interested in everything we could tell him about Kenya. He enjoyed talking to

Gikonyo Kiano, whom we had invited to meet him, asked many questions about the current situation and future prospects for Africans, and kept us laughing with a rich store of jokes.

Architect and inventor Buckminster Fuller quite unexpectedly also came to dinner one night. Bob's job often required him to meet visiting Americans at the airport, but due to a mix-up he had only a half-hour's notice of Mr. Fuller's arrival. After dashing out of the city through noontime traffic, he reached the terminal just as the plane was landing. He took Mr. Fuller out to lunch and on a tour of the Game Park and then delivered him to a sundowner at the Norfolk Hotel, where Mr. Fuller had been invited to lecture and show slides to a group of Nairobi architects.

Bob remembers how bored the audience seemed at first, and how disdainful of this American architect who thought he could tell them something they didn't already know. But as Mr. Fuller warmed to his subject and showed slides that illustrated his ideas, they began to sit up and take notice. By the end of the lecture they couldn't wait to crowd around him with their excited comments and questions.

Our phone was out of order that day, a not unusual condition, but Bob had somehow found time to race home late in the afternoon to tell me not to wait dinner, as he didn't know when he would be back. About nine-thirty that night I was reading by the fire when Bob turned up with Mr. Fuller. They were both famished. By the time the lecture had ended, it was too late for dinner at the Norfolk and most Nairobi restaurants were closed. Bob didn't know what to do with Mr. Fuller except bring him home.

Marikus and Ali had gone to bed, so I foraged in the kitchen. A search revealed some canned goods and a few meager salad fixings. I got together a light supper that included canned Kenya baked beans (for Mr. Fuller, a Bostonian!), long skinny Kenya hot dogs, and Lyon's ice cream (always a bit flat from its long sojourn on a ship from England) topped by some of our precious Hershey's chocolate syrup. Mr. Fuller graciously declared that he loved hot dogs and that everything tasted wonderful. He must have been really hungry.

Between bites he held us spellbound on every subject from his invention of the geodesic dome to his ideas about education and the nature of the universe. In one flight of imagination he proposed to solve the housing shortage and lack of space in Tokyo by building a city floating on platforms anchored in Tokyo Bay. Mathematics fascinated him, and he frequently illustrated a point with a mathematical example. He said he could teach a young child spherical trigonometry, provided he could have that child before he became entrapped in the rigidity of the regular school curriculum. Fuller believed schools too often restrict a child's thinking, closing off the creative vents that allow new and original ideas to emerge.

I remember he expounded, too, on his theory that Africa was populated by Polynesians who migrated across the Indian Ocean, and cited some common characteristics of the cultures. Elderly, rotund, white-haired and slightly deaf, he may have looked unprepossessing, but his mind raced along such extraordinary paths that you forgot his appearance and were caught up in the excitement of his ideas, carried along by the imaginative ramblings of a man who was surely a genius.

These kinds of experiences with visitors from America and elsewhere, as well as with local Kenyans, added richness and depth to our two years in Kenya. They provided opportunities to become acquainted and to exchange ideas informally with some of the leading figures from our own country and others. We were crossing paths with people from many levels of society and government and from many walks of life, and gaining a perspective on the world far beyond what we had known in our years in married student housing or on that suburban street near Washington. Certainly I had never expected to meet, much less entertain, such a wide spectrum of distinguished visitors. I sometimes found myself marveling at how our lives had changed—mine in particular, from an insular suburban existence to this. It was exciting and stimulating, this life we were leading. Most of the time I threw myself enthusiastically into the constant round of coffees and cocktail parties, luncheons and tea parties and dinners. But there were times when I realized that although I was willing to do this, even enjoy it, for two years, I wouldn't want to devote my entire life to large scale entertaining and being entertained. At some point I would want something more, want my life to count for something beyond this social whirl.

Cathy and Robbie, too, were having to adapt to the many changes in their lives. In a strange country, surrounded by a fascinating but alien culture, they were faced with making new friends, adjusting to new teachers and a new school with unfamiliar ways. They were also experiencing a different kind of home life, with four servants and far more entertaining than we had ever done in the States—frequent out-of-town visitors and houseguests, "official" cocktail parties and dinners, informal gatherings of friends. On the many occasions when we had overnight guests, Kelly moved into Cathy and Robbie's "dormitory" and her room became the guestroom. Her bed was often still warm from the last visitor when we had to whip off the sheets and prepare for the next.

It made for an interesting but hectic life, and sometimes I tired of it. An evening at home, sitting quietly by the fire and reading, or a Sunday spent with only the family, became a rare treat. Instead of alternating their days off, I began having Ali and Marikus both take Sundays off, along with Rachel, so we could have the house to ourselves. I enjoyed cooking dinner with the children's and Bob's help, even enjoyed washing the dishes alone—though in truth, if I was tired, I sometimes stacked them for Marikus to do in the morning.

The numerous visitors and frenetic social activity, combined with the adjustments to life in Kenya, occasionally intensified family problems. Cathy was ricocheting into her rebellious teen years and in Africa, we found, this could lead to unusual complications.

One night, as we were leaving for a cocktail party at the Consul General's (a command performance that included bringing the devilled eggs and cocktail meatballs that Marikus and I had labored over all afternoon) Cathy confronted us at the door. She had been invited to a dance by a boy she had met at a recent party, and she wanted to know if she could go. Bob and I suggested we talk about it later, but she demanded an answer then and there.

We didn't have anything against the boy except that he was eighteen and the dance was his senior prom. Cathy may have looked almost eighteen, but she was only twelve. We would have said no anywhere—Africa, America, or wherever.

Cathy stomped up to her room and slammed the door. I stood for a moment, looking after this tall daughter whose figure had blossomed in a few short months, and whose honey-blond hair, no longer slicked back into a ponytail, now framed her face in soft, becoming curls. She was growing up too fast.

Sighing, I followed Bob out the door, along with our houseguest, Steve Low from the Uganda Consulate, and my twelve dozen devilled eggs and five hundred meatballs. An hour later I was summoned to the phone by the Consul General's wife, Jane. Robbie was on the other end, and he was crying.

"Mom....Cathy ran away!" he sobbed.

I promised him we would be right home and went to find Bob. When we excused ourselves to Consul General Dudley Withers and Jane, they were understanding. Many times I thanked my good fortune at having someone like Jane as the "boss's wife." Though she had no children of her own, she made it clear that family considerations came first, that the needs of our children had priority over diplomatic duties, which she never seemed to take very seriously anyway. I had met her at a party at the Residence the day after we arrived in Kenya, and she had said, "Oh, forget making that formal call. Now that we've met, that's all that matters! Let me know what I can do to help you get settled."

Jane was a refreshing change from what I had been led to expect in Washington about life in the diplomatic service. I think she was probably quite unusual—a warm, informal hostess who spent hours each day playing her piano while on week-ends Dudley tinkered in overalls with his MG out in the garage. Not the stereotypical, protocol-conscious diplomatic couple.

Luckily the Consul General's residence on Muthaiga Road was only a couple of miles from our house. We scrambled into our car and drove toward home, the headlights probing the blackness ahead. We hadn't gone far before the lights picked out a figure moving toward us, hunched over the handlebars of a bike. It was Cathy, alone in the African night, with her nighty in a doll's suitcase and twenty shillings she had taken from my purse. She was crying, and she was scared. She resisted getting into the station wagon at first, but we finally persuaded her to let us take her home. Calming her down also took a while, but she did finally agree not to run away again, at least not in Africa.

That weekend lives in my memory as one of the more stressful times I spent in Kenya. It was also a time when Cathy eloquently revealed the child/woman she was. She herself was aware of the metamorphosis occurring within her. One day, half-humorous and half-tearful, she looked down at her developing figure and wailed, "Here I am with this child's mind in this woman's body, and I don't know what to do!"

The weekend of her childish attempt to run away was the same weekend when, without warning, she had to fill my shoes as hostess and helpmate to her father. She came through with flying colors. We had been asked by Consul General Withers to give a dinner party the next night for some visiting National War College people. I woke up in the morning feverish and aching with what turned out to be Asian flu. Ali, Marikus, Bob, and our houseguest Steve all pitched in to prepare the dinner while I, through the fog in my brain, tried to orchestrate their efforts from my bed.

Cathy's contribution came later, when she stood at the door with Bob greeting our guests, making introductions, then circulating with hors d'oeuvres. At dinner she sat in my place and helped Bob serve, chatting with colonels and ambassadors with the poise of a veteran hostess. The experiences she had in Africa, the wide spectrum of people she met, helped develop in her, I believe, a warmth and empathy for all kinds of people that has stayed with her to this day.

The flip side is that Foreign Service children who are away too long from the United States sometimes end up neither fish nor fowl. We had seen this happen in other families. The children lose their sense of American identity and feel they belong nowhere. Cathy was fortunate that she had those two adventurous years to widen her experience with the world and its people, but underneath the solid bedrock of an American childhood and a strong sense of her American roots.

Interesting and exotic as East Africa was for all of us, though, it was often scary, especially for Robbie. Kelly was too young to be much affected. Her family was her security, and as long as we were there, she was happy. For Cathy, at the mercy of her hormones, Kenya was merely the setting for her stormy entry into adolescence—interesting but secondary. She seemed oblivious of the menacing shadows that haunted Robbie.

Bats flying through the stairwell, geckos sliding across the ceilings, and most of all the nightlong din of nocturnal noises from outside the windows frightened him. He became a ten-year-old insomniac, coming to stand by my bedside in the middle of the night, waiting for me to sense his presence and open my eyes. Many a night I took him back to his room and sat with him until he slept, trying to soothe and reassure him, though at the same time I knew some of his fears were justified.

There were, it was true, wild animals outside in the forest, though the windows of our house were barred against them. Barred, too, against people: the few remaining Mau Mau terrorists still being hunted down in the highlands, and the "pole-fishers" who came in the night. With their long poles they fished through the window gratings for wallets, watches, and jewelry left lying on bureaus.

One night we almost had a break-in. Bob and I were asleep in the first-floor master bedroom when something awakened me. I opened my eyes to see two heads silhouetted in the window against the bright moonlight that illuminated the garden.

I froze, my heart pumping wildly, then reached out and shook Bob, urgently whispering his name. By the time he came to, the heads had disappeared. Bob called the police, who searched the grounds thoroughly, torches flashing among the trees while we and the children watched. Our dog Chumley slept blissfully through it all, not even blinking an eye when the police roared up to the door and fanned out through the woods.

We had agreed to adopt Chomondeley (shortened to Chumley) from our predecessors. He was a big, dumb golden retriever with the unattractive habit of carrying a large muddy rock around in his mouth. At the sight of us turning into the driveway he would drop the rock and race toward us, then lick us ecstatically as we got out of the car, painting our faces with muddy tongue-strokes and leaving surrealistic smears of thick red mud mixed with drool on our clothing and legs. The night of our attempted break-in, had the intruders succeeded in gaining entrance to the house, they would have had to step over our "watchdog" Chumley, dead to the world on the floor in the hall.

Despite their careful search the police found no one that night, but for a few weeks even Bob and I slept uneasily, afraid of a second attempt. It became one more thing for Robbie to worry about. He knew there were health hazards, too. He had been stung by wild bees, warned about bilharzia, took malaria pills weekly. And despite my precautions of washing vegetables and fruits in purple baths of potassium permanganate to kill the parasites, and serving the good Kenya beef well-done to guard against tapeworm, he and Bob both had frequent bouts of gastroenteritis. He had also had a particularly frightening experience with a wild monkey.

He had begun collecting animals almost as soon as we got to Kenya. At the Norfolk, he had spent much of his time climbing one of the palm trees and having conversations with a tame parrot, or chasing lizards around, trying to catch them in an envelope. When we visited the Coryndon Museum (now the National Museum of Kenya) he was mesmerized by the displays of venomous snakes slithering around in a series of deep open pits.

His room in our house in Muthaiga housed a cage of white mice and another with two guinea hens, and out near the servants' quarters were our growing flock of chickens and four rabbits in a hutch, given him by friends. He had also been begging for a pet monkey. Small troops of them sometimes traveled across our garden at treetop level, but they were shy and elusive, and we caught only occasional glimpses of them high in the trees. In a rash moment, Bob and I told Robbie, half jokingly, that he could have one if he caught it himself. It had seemed a safe enough promise at the time.

I was rolling out piecrust one afternoon when Robbie came running into the kitchen. He had been playing in a neighbor's garden and was out of breath and excited.

"Mom! Can I have a banana? There's a monkey on the Ainscows' veranda roof, and I want to try to catch it!"

He brushed his brown hair out of his eyes and wiped perspiration from his face with an impatient hand. His blue school uniform shirt had come untucked from his jeans, which he invariably changed into the minute he got home from school. He hated the gray school shorts that were part of the uniform. Cold knees didn't bother him, but at the advanced age of ten, baring them did. In the States he had long ago graduated into long pants.

"We're all out of bananas, Rob. Sorry," I said.

"Aw…well, how 'bout bread? Can I try some bread?"

"I guess—though I don't know if monkeys like bread."

"Thanks, Mom!" And he was gone.

I went on crimping the rim of the pastry, wondering if the Ainscows were home and what we would do with the monkey in the unlikely event that Robbie actually caught it. Moments later he was standing in the doorway, sobbing and holding his arm.

"He bit me, Mom!" he cried between sobs. "The monkey bit me. Look!"

Blood trickled from ugly tooth marks on his forearm. Grabbing a towel I pressed it against the wound with one hand while I dialed Patience Davies, then Bob's office, with the other. We had found Dr. Davies—British-born, British-trained, and the only pediatrician in Kenya—while we were still at the Norfolk, when Kelly had a fever. We and most Americans in Nairobi entrusted our children to her and were eternally thankful that she was there. Tall, plain, with a warm smile and a brisk, reassuring manner, she had a habit of peering intently into a sick child'e eyes and saying, "Yes, but how do you feel <u>inside</u> yourself?" It included the child as a partner in her mysterious medical world, and the answer often seemed to help in her diagnosis.

While we waited for the doctor, Robbie told me, his voice shaking, what had happened. He had been standing by the Ainscows' veranda, holding the bread in his hand, and the next thing he knew the monkey had leaped down off the roof, grabbed the bread, and jumped back up in a flash. Robbie had looked down to see blood running down his arm

He was pale and trembling. I thought he might be in shock.

Dr. Davies was there in minutes, with Bob not far behind. She gave Robbie a massive shot of penicillin, explaining as she bandaged his arm that next to man a monkey has the dirtiest mouth and most dangerous bite of any animal. There were three tooth marks, one of them very deep.

"I'm afraid there will be a nasty infection," she warned. "And there's the chance of something worse. The monkey was not acting normally. They don't ordinarily leave the troop and go off on their own. It might just be a maverick, of course. Or it could have rabies."

Rabies! The word conjured up nightmarish visions of mad dogs and mouth-frothing convulsions. If the monkey was infected, Dr. Davies said, Robbie would need a long series of painful and dangerous injections.

"There's only one way to find out. Find someone to shoot it," she suggested. "They can examine the brain for rabies at the government lab in Kabete."

If the monkey couldn't be found we would have to proceed with the dreaded injections. When I went to tell Jill Ainscow what had happened, she said that after the monkey bit Robbie, it actually came into her house and tried to attack her little daughter, who was Kelly's age. The monkey was still hanging around their garden, so Jill called a friend, a hunter who obligingly came and shot it. I put the carcass in a brown paper bag, and Robbie and I drove the few miles to Kabete where we handed it over to a white-coated Indian technician.

Bob and I tried to conceal our anxiety from each other, but I went to bed that night with dread a hard lump in my stomach. I was haunted by images of disease-carrying snails, warlike safari ants, wild bees, and rabid monkeys. My imagined nightmares about Africa had not been just fantasies after all.

Fortunately, our anxiety about rabies was unfounded and, blessedly, short-lived. Twenty-four hours after Robbie and I dropped off the carcass, we had the verdict: negative! As Dr. Davies had predicted, however, in spite of penicillin the bite was badly infected. Robbie's arm swelled to twice its size and turned a sickly yellow with angry streaks of red and green running from wrist to elbow. Dr. Davies came by daily to check on it, and I was kept busy applying hot compresses. After several days the wound opened and drained great torrents of green pus. Finally, it began to heal.

By now Robbie was beginning to feel rather pleased with himself for having had such an adventure. After all, as Bob told him, how many kids can say they have been attacked and bitten by a wild monkey? But I noticed that there was no more talk of having one as a pet.

Still, the night terrors sometimes returned to keep him awake until dawn, listening for the first sounds of morning: the rattling and clanking of the garbage truck; then the boy delivering milk to the front door, his bicycle tires crunching on the gravel and the triangular tetrapaks of milk slapping wetly on the step; and finally, the comforting everyday sound of the gardener hosing down the car under the bedroom window. For a relieved ten-year-old, it was another night conquered and survived.

13

VENTURING FORTH: NEW ROLES

If during the first months in Nairobi I had sometimes felt like a lost soul, robbed of my usual roles and with empty time on my hands, that soon changed as new activities filled my days. Many of them involved children, either ours or others.'

Gloria Hagburg asked me to fill in for her in a volunteer job that brought me in contact with African teenagers. At African Girls' High School in Kikuyu, an Irish woman doctor and a Scottish nurse volunteered their services to give the students periodic physicals. My task was to take a brief history; fill in a chart with name, age, tribe, height, and weight; test each girl's vision; and check for a vaccination. The doctor and nurse then examined the girls and had them leave urine and stool specimens to be tested for Africa's rampant parasites.

One by one in their crisp green school uniforms they came into the little room where I sat. Their English was excellent; they answered my questions in the shy, soft voices I had come to expect from East African women and girls, their words carefully articulated with a marked English accent and lilt. But my attempts at small talk fell flat.

"So, Warimu, you are Kikuyu. Is your home near here?" I would ask. A bashful smile and a shake of the close-cropped head.

"Where then?"

"Nyeri," Warimu might reply.

"Nyeri! How often do you get home?" A shrug of the shoulders and perhaps a giggle.

It was difficult to make contact with these downcast eyes, and it is amazing how hard it is to converse without it. But something good was happening here, shyness notwithstanding. The school shone like a beacon in the void that was African education in Kenya, especially secondary education for girls. Established by the Church of Scotland as a mission school, African Girls' High was a model of what the colonial government could have accomplished, but didn't, all over Kenya. For a long time the school was supported solely by the Church and with the hard work of the dedicated missionaries who ran it. By 1958 it was being meagerly funded by the government, though still staffed by a Scottish headmistress and faculty of European missionaries. They kept it going on a shoestring, but nevertheless provided African girls with a fine education and a different life from the one they had known in their villages: airy dormitories; bright modern classrooms; neat, attractive grounds with green lawns and flower beds; and knowledge of a world beyond Kenya's borders.

It never failed to amaze Bob and me that the school curriculum in Kenya was so British in its content and orientation. African children who had never seen an oak tree or a robin were required to learn about English trees and birds; memorize the names of English kings and queens; compute their math problems in English pounds, shillings and pence (different from East African money); and study English literature. It required a prodigious feat of memory to master such a broad body of knowledge about things totally unfamiliar in order to pass the all-important school examinations. It also seemed incongruous that, surrounded by the strange and wonderful flowers, trees, animals, and insects of Africa, as well as the rich heritage of tribal lore and folk stories, African children were learning nothing about them. One of the first things the African government of independent Kenya undertook was a complete revision and "Africanization" of the school curriculum, though at the same time retaining many elements of the British education so highly esteemed for so long by East Africans.

Though the graduates of African Girls' High were only a handful out of millions of uneducated girls, they were an example of what could be achieved when a commitment was made to education, and opportunities extended to attend a good school. These girls became part of a new generation of African women who left head straps and goatskins behind and plunged triumphantly into the 20th Century. Many of them went on to college in the States. Some became teachers and later served as headmistresses of this and other high schools. Others moved into business and the professions, and ran everything from government agencies, clinics, and hotels to offices and tea farms. All were enabled to do so partly because of the education they had received at African Girls' High and the poise and self-confidence they had developed there. Unfortunately, because of the lack of schools, for a number of years women like these were a very small minority.

I met another group of African girls when a local cosmetics firm agreed to sponsor the first-ever fashion show in Kenya with African models. The emphasis was on European styles, though some traditional African garments, as well as a few saris, were included. The proceeds went toward scholarships for some of the college students going overseas. Ruth Njiiri and Ernestine Kiano were among those helping to organize the show, and Ernestine asked me to join her as a co-fashion "expert." We spent several days outfitting and grooming several of the models, girls who knew Ernestine and had enlisted her help. In the bedroom of an English friend, amid piles of lingerie and dresses and a welter of hats and gloves, we gave advice about which styles and colors were becoming and what accessories were needed. I loaned a pair of my shoes to one of the girls, a crinoline of Cathy's to another, and some costume jewelry to a third. We coached the girls on how to stand and how to walk, as they had no idea what to do on a runway. In this intimate setting they forgot to be shy and began clowning around, caricaturing a model's strut, swinging their hips and rolling their eyes until we were all laughing.

Two of them were Kikuyu, so to get them back to business, I risked one of the Kikuyu phrases I had learned: "*Nituthii* (Let's get going)!" A moment of surprised silence, then more laughter and an answering flood of Kikuyu greeted my brave foray into their language.

Because of a prior commitment I wasn't able to be at the "fashion parade," as the local press called it, but Ernestine reported that it was a great success. "Our girls outshone them all," she said proudly.

Not all my teen-aged friends were Africans. At a dinner party I met an Englishwoman who was active in the Girl Guides of Kenya. When she mentioned the need for leaders I asked if I could help with an African company. My Swahili was not fluent enough for that, she said, but she was looking for someone to take over the Muthaiga Girl Guides—all Europeans, of course. Two other American women had volunteered to lead the Muthaiga troop of Brownies, but she hadn't been able to find anyone willing to be Girl Guide captain.

So Cathy and I became Girl Guides, and with our company of English girls we tied knots, worked on badges, and picnicked in the Ngong Hills and the Game Park. Hiking and camping farther out in the bush had been banned since the outbreak of the Mau Mau Emergency, though by 1958 there was probably little risk of attack.

Our company met at the Muthaiga School, close beside the main road from Nairobi to Thika. Every few minutes a truck thundered by, blotting out all other sound. Cathy, whose classroom was on that side of the school, said it was like that all day. Her teacher, Mrs. Davidson, was obliged to stop the lessons every time a truck passed, and no wonder. Lacking glass panes, the windows were nothing more than openings in the cement block walls intended to let in light and air. Instead they funneled in the traffic noise and admitted precious little light, especially in the gray gloom of the rainy seasons. Nor could the classroom be brightened by the flick of a switch, since there was no electricity in the school. In order to see well enough to tie knots and play games we held most of our meetings outdoors unless it was pouring rain. I couldn't imagine how the children could see to do their schoolwork during the day.

The girls, all English except Cathy, threw themselves enthusiastically into our activities. They were touchingly appreciative of our time together. In spite of their privileged lives, they seemed lonely. Apparently their families seldom did things together—safaris, swimming, picnics—the way we Americans did. When I asked other mothers to drive on a field trip or help at a meeting, they were generally too busy. Tennis and golf monopolized a lot of their time and energies. The girls were often left with the servants. Many expected to be sent "home" soon to boarding school in England. Their brothers had long since departed, usually by the age of seven or eight. They "came out" to Kenya on holiday once or twice a year. Robbie's two English friends next door, Nigel and Bruce, were sent away to boarding school at the ripe old ages of eight and nine. Their mother wept for days before and after their departure, but their father was adamant. He would not allow the boys to remain at home to be "molly-coddled." Boarding school, he firmly believed, would turn them into proper little Englishmen. Because the boys were sent away so young, girls dominated the classrooms of government schools like Muthaiga after Standard (Grade) Four, just biding their time until they too would fly away to England.

Not all of the girls in my Guide Company were poor little rich girls. Mandy was a poor little poor girl, a mousy waif who lived out Thika Road, far from Muthaiga. She rode to and from school in a truck driven by a man who she said was not her father. She was vague about their relationship—an uncle? friend? Often she had no school uniform to wear, and came in what looked like hand-me-downs—a soiled skirt trailing to her ankles, a bedraggled sweater with the elbows out. Her lank hair hung in strings; dark eyes stared from a sallow face.

I wondered about her family. How had they come to be in Kenya? Had her father, or uncle, been in the British Army, a lorry driver perhaps, who decided to stay on in East Africa after his hitch in the Army was over? No one at school seemed to know any more about them than I did.

On Guide days Mandy had no way to get home after meetings, so I drove her out Thika Road and dropped her off where a muddy, rock-strewn track trailed off into the bush. When I offered to drive her farther she said no, the road was too bad. Sometimes her mother, holding a baby, with toddlers wrapped around her legs, was waiting for Mandy by the road. She would return my greeting with a brief "Thank you, mum," then hand the baby to Mandy and turn away and trudge up the track. They lived in a mud-and-wattle house, Mandy said, a long way from the main road.

When the girls passed their tests and were ready to don Guide uniforms, the material had to be ordered and the dresses made by a *fundi*. Mandy asked to speak to me after a meeting.

"I can't get a uniform, Captain Stephens. My mum hasn't got the money for material." Embarrassed, she wouldn't look at me.

"Don't worry, Mandy," I said. "I'm having Cathy's and my uniforms made, and I got extra material, so I'll just go ahead and have one made for you too."

The thin shoulders straightened a little. She smiled. "Thank you, Captain Stephens!"

For a few weeks she seemed more a part of the group, clad in her blue uniform like all the others. Then, without warning, she disappeared.

"Someone said they moved down to the coast," Headmaster Peter Toy told me.

"No," claimed Mandy's teacher. "The kids say they went back to the UK."

The family had vanished apparently without a trace, leaving their mud-and-wattle house to return to the earth from which it came. Mandy's fate, like the deaths of Petro's mother, remained another of Africa's mysteries.

At Muthaiga School, I took on other volunteer jobs. The Parents' Association was always in need of help, with fund-raising "fetes" and Sports Days and teas. At one of the fetes I had the bad luck to be assigned to selling tickets at the tea tent and was kept busy all afternoon struggling to make change in East African shillings and pence. Meanwhile the children rode ponies and a merry-go-round to the music of the regimental band of the K.S.L.I.—the King's Shropshire Light Infantry with the gloriously British name that sounded as though it were being said through a mouthful of mashed potatoes.

Ours was one of only three American families whose children attended Muthaiga School. The rest of the students and the staff were British. Teaching methods and curriculum, like those at African Girls' High, were British. Our children learned British history, read British literature, had to master the intricacies of multiplication and long division using English pounds, shillings and pence. A money system not based on decimals, it was so complex that the solution to a simple long division problem covered a full sheet of paper. Cathy and Robbie and I wrestled over "maths" homework together each night.

Handwriting presented difficulties too. Robbie, in the throes of learning cursive writing, American style, had suddenly to relearn the formation of letters like small l (no loop) and small a (open at the top, like u). His handwriting never recovered.

The children started each day with an assembly in the open-sided thatched *banda* in front of the school, where Mr. Toy led them in singing and intoned a short prayer. Back in their classrooms they rose to their feet politely whenever a teacher entered the room. Cathy's Standard Six teacher Mrs. Davidson, a Scotswoman of formidable stature and personality, would sail majestically into the classroom each morning, saying in her thick Scottish burr, "Good morrrrrning, gettles and boys!" Cathy's imitation of her was perfect.

Mrs. Davidson was old-fashioned and strict. Cathy reported that she sometimes slapped children who didn't behave. She also did not approve of America or Americans and took pains to point out our shortcomings at every opportunity. Cathy endured this with admirable fortitude, I thought, and even got a perverse kind of enjoyment out of fending off the barbs.

"Well, Cathleen," Mrs. Davidson said on one occasion. "I see you Americans have been stirring up trouble again, entertaining Tom Mboya in the States!"

"Yes, Mrs. Davidson," Cathy answered. "He was telling us all about his trip when he came to dinner last night!" Touché, Cathy!

Gradually, though, she and Mrs. Davidson developed great mutual respect and in the end, according to Cathy, became quite fond of each other.

Headmaster Peter Toy did like Americans and relied on the three American mothers for much of the volunteer work at the school. When one of them offered the use of her family's pool, I helped Mr. Toy teach swimming. Every Friday afternoon we drove groups of school children to a coffee farm in Kiambu, where I took the beginners at the shallow end of the pool while Mr. Toy worked with the more advanced swimmers. We ended the school week happily kicking and splashing in the bright African sunshine. Some of the children even learned to swim a little.

After almost nine months in Kenya, it was hard to remember sometimes how empty my days had seemed when I first arrived, how useless I had felt, floundering in this new environment, trying to find where and how I fit in. Now my days were crowded and passed too quickly. I wanted time to slow down so I could savor them. I had begun to feel comfortable here, a part of the life around me.

Once unfamiliar words and phrases fell easily from my lips*: samosas, asante sana, kahawa, tafadhali, chai.*

"Ni nakwenda Nairobi leo," I would call to Ali, not stopping to think whether I was telling him in English or Swahili that I was going to Nairobi today.

I had unconsciously adopted some "Englishisms" too. Traffic circles had become roundabouts, trucks were lorries, four o'clock in the afternoon was automatically time for tea.

Kenya would never really be home; I didn't truly belong here. But many things about this country that had seemed so foreign and strange were becoming everyday familiar, fitting me almost as naturally as my own skin. Even so, I occasionally had spells of homesickness, especially when I knew the seasons were changing at home. I missed spring in Washington, cherry blossoms, red autumn leaves, the smell of the ocean at the New Jersey shore. The nostalgic moments passed quickly, though. I was too busy to linger long on thoughts of home.

14

SOLO SAFARI

When August came, Nairobi was cold and gray. My mood reflected the gloomy weather. A wire had come from Bob's mother that his father was gravely ill. Bob had flown home to Michigan immediately and had arrived two days before his father died. He was staying on for a short while with his mother.

I grieved sadly for both of them, and for Pop. I also felt very alone. Bob and I didn't even have the solace of talking to each other. International phone calls were rare back then, especially from Kenya, where phone service was unreliable and long distance calls prohibitively expensive. Even official communications went back and forth via cable or in the diplomatic pouch. Bob and I, too, had to rely on cables.

Meanwhile the school term ended and August holidays began. We had planned to spend them at the coast and months before had booked rooms at the Eden Roc Hotel in Malindi. Huddled by the living room fire that Ali kept burning day and night, feeling lonely and vulnerable without Bob, I debated what to do. Cathy and Robbie had already moped around for several days. The reality of their grandfather's death, ten thousand miles away, was hard for them to grasp, and even harder to know how to deal with. It was their first intimate experience with death—and mine, too—but intimacy far removed by geographical distance. Without family around, and none of the final rituals that usually surround death, we floundered through the hours and days. Even Kelly, only three, sensed that something was wrong and tagged forlornly around after me. Malindi's sunshine and warmth sounded healing; maybe some time there would cheer us up.

The prospect of doing this on my own—driving more than three hundred miles on an unfamiliar rough dirt road through uninhabited bush country, alone with the children—was daunting. This would be the first long safari our family had taken, and I would be doing it without Bob. It wasn't people I was afraid of. Despite my initial nervousness about Mau Mau, the open friendliness and warmth of nearly everyone I had met in Kenya had quickly dispelled any fears I might have had. But large wild animals and the possibility of car trouble out in the bush were something else again

I lay sleepless at night, wrestling with my ever-present reluctance to take risks, and wondering what Bob would say. He had often joked that he sometimes had to drag me kicking and screaming into new experiences, and I knew there was more than a little truth in that. The question was, could I drag myself into this one?

In the end the allure of an escape to Malindi was too much. I woke up one morning determined to go. Bob could join us when he returned to Kenya. Ali had already planned to take his annual leave and would go with us to visit his family. I welcomed the idea of his company, but since he didn't have a license, he wouldn't be able to help with the driving. Nor did he know anything about the inner workings of a car. In the event of mechanical trouble, he and I would be equally helpless.

When Ali first came to work for us, he told us that his greatest ambition in life was to become a chauffeur. He had begged Bob to teach him to drive. Bob agreed to try. After several sessions of patient instruction and practice in our driveway, he seemed ready for the road. I watched the two of them take off down Karura Avenue with Ali at the wheel. Grinning gleefully, he gave the jeep the gas and went crashing through the frangipani trees along the verge and into a stone wall. The fender was crumpled, the axle was bent, and Bob's nerves were shattered. He offered on the spot to pay for professional driving lessons for Ali.

For several weeks Ali went off each day after lunch to the driving school in town. Finally he announced that he was ready for his road test. He took it three times and failed each time. Apparently he just couldn't get the knack of it, no matter how hard he tried, and he never did get his license. On our safari to Malindi he would be able to offer only general encouragement and his own cheerful presence in the front seat beside me.

I took the car to the local garage for a safari check, had the tank filled with petrol, and that same morning, before I could change my mind, we were off. A few miles out of Nairobi we left greenness and flowers behind. The road, increasingly rough, began its slow, three-hundred-mile descent through scorching bush to the Indian Ocean. Cathy and Robbie had to hang on to anything they could grab in order not to be thrown out of their seats. Kelly was strapped in her car seat beside them, her blond head wobbling with each bump. Neither of the older children, innocently trusting, showed any anxiety about embarking on this adventure with just Ali and me. I seemed to be the only one with qualms about the risks we were taking.

As the hours went by, it got hotter and hotter. Sweat poured into my eyes; blisters began to form on my hands where I gripped the wheel. Cathy and Robbie continued to hang on grimly in the back seat, too hot and dusty and uncomfortable even to argue with each other. Kelly amused herself by singing and talking to her doll. When I looked in the rearview mirror, I could see her lips moving, though I couldn't hear much over the noise of the engine and the whoosh of air through the windows.

Slowly the needle on the gas gauge edged down to empty. There were no petrol stations before the rest stop at Mtito Andei, a tiny pinprick on the map midway to the coast. Around each bend in the road and beyond every slight rise, I expected to see some sign of civilization, but there was none—only tan plains and stunted thorn trees. Sometimes I glimpsed a baobab tree, huge trunk squatting on the horizon, short twisted branches thrust like aerial roots toward the sky.

Ali roused himself and tried to reassure me. "Is coming soon, memsahib. *Bado kidogo*—in a little while."

Anxiously I eyed the gas gauge and scanned the road ahead, glancing at the bush on either side. Earlier in the day we had met another car every half-hour or so, but for the past two hours we had seen none. We were not far from Tsavo, a large semi-arid reserve where in future years poachers would cruelly reduce the populations of great game animals. But in 1958 Tsavo was still known for its huge numbers of elephants, lions, and rhinos. The last thing I wanted was to run out of petrol in this barren stretch of country well populated with big game. I prayed I wouldn't meet up with a rhino or anything else. Ali and I were, needless to say, unarmed. In the wake of Mau Mau, carrying guns was illegal in Kenya, and anyway, I wouldn't have known what to do with a gun if I had had one. And what would I do if I actually did run out of petrol? The mechanic in Nairobi had assured me I had enough to get to Mtito Andei, but what if he was wrong? How many hours would we have to sit, alone and unprotected in this brutal heat, before help might come along? What if it got dark and no one came?

My unease was edging into panic when we finally saw the small cluster of buildings at Mtito Andei, alone in the bush with the British flag flying bravely in front. Beautiful sight! We got out, stretched our legs, had the car filled with petrol, used the bathrooms, and bought drinks and snacks: the inevitable orange squash, sickly sweet and warm, but blessedly wet, and packets of curried peas, satisfyingly salted and crunchy.

Somewhat revived, I headed the car once more toward the Indian Ocean. The afternoon trailed on and on, as though time were a rubber band endlessly stretching, creating a day that would last forever. I was very tired. I thought of Bob, so far away in America, and longed for his reassuring presence beside me. Malindi and a cooling sea began to seem like some unattainable African Land of Oz that I would never reach.

I glanced behind me. Kelly had finally dozed off in spite of the jouncing. Cathy and Robbie clung to the back of my seat, peering anxiously ahead. They had given up asking the eternal question, Are we almost there? I think they too wondered if we were to travel on through Africa forever.

Ali continued to offer assurances, though he was vague about how much farther it might be. It was almost dusk when the dry plains began to give way to the welcome sight of coconut palms and banana trees, fanned by the trade winds and swaying amidst fields of sugar cane. The lush greens of trees and cane washed over me like cool rain, the vivid colors almost an assault on my eyes after hours of squinting through the dust.

At Kilifi I drove the car onto the ferry, a large wooden raft drawn across the river by several men pulling on ropes from the opposite bank. Numb from the long drive, I cruised slowly through the last few coastal villages of square mud houses where men squatted under the thatch, drinking beer in the swinging light of kerosene lanterns.

As we rolled into Malindi a full moon rose out of the Indian Ocean. The trade winds blew steadily, rustling through the palms. A kind of exultation filled me. Not just relief that we had made the trip safely through three hundred miles of empty bush. For perhaps the first time I could remember, I had made a completely independent decision, had acted upon it, had successfully carried it out.

Before I was married, while I was in high school and college, my parents had helped me decide about summer jobs, about choosing a college, picking a major. After Bob and I were married, we had decided most things together. I had always had someone to consult with. There hadn't been many opportunities to act on my own. Up to now I hadn't particularly questioned this. It was pretty standard for women of my generation, when the accepted goal, given a powerful urgency by World War II, was to get married and have children. Feminism and the turmoil of ideas it generated were still somewhere in the future.

But our safe arrival in Malindi was an intoxicating moment, the beginning of my realization that I could be, wanted to be, more than a wife and mother, that I was, after all, willing to take risks, to try new things. I didn't know it then, but I had taken the first tentative step on a new path.

That night in Malindi, I only knew that this daylong safari had left me with a feeling of satisfaction and accomplishment. Ahead lay tea, a bath, then dinner. Life was good.

A Malindi vacation meant sun, sea, sand, sleep, two weeks of rest and relax-
ation, and a chance to grieve quietly for Pop. The pace of life slowed to allow
afternoon naps, plenty of reading, frequent swims, and leisurely strolls on the
beach. Several times Ali rode in on his bicycle from his outlying village, bringing
us gifts of coconuts from his *shamba*. It was a comfort to see his familiar face and
cheerful smile in this place where I knew no one.

During our first week at the Coast, the children and I several times walked
into the sleepy little Arab village of Malindi. It bore traces of a dwindling Arab
culture: crumbling coral stone houses, a small white mosque, a few black-veiled
Arab women and swarthy men in white robes, turbaned sailors on the dhows.
The flag of Oman and Zanzibar still flew above the little courthouse, and a few
miles down the road lay the mossy ruins of Gede, once thought to have been an
Arab city but now known to have been a 12th century Swahili town. As we
strolled among the vine-shrouded stone walls and foundations, I imagined the
arrival along this coast, five hundred years earlier, of the Portuguese explorer,
Vasco da Gama. For the next two hundred years the Portuguese ruled the coastal
strip with a ruthless hand. British historian Basil Davidson has called this "a time
of ruin" for Malindi, Mombasa, and other coastal city-states, as the Portuguese
drained them of their riches like "men who squeeze lemons for their juice."
When the Portuguese were finally ousted in the 18th century, new over-
lords—Arabs from Oman—took control, and even when we vacationed in Malindi in 1958 their sultan, by special arrangement with the British government,
still ruled the coast from his palace in Zanzibar.

But for hundreds of years, since before the centuries of occupation, a Swahili
culture and a Swahili people, born of Arab and African intermarriage, had flour-
ished here. In this part of East Africa known to the Greeks as Azania and to the
Arabs as Zanj, the Swahili language developed and became part of Kenya's, and
much of Africa's, heritage. Its written literature included a wealth of poems and
songs and stories, and Swahili architecture contributed the graceful style of coral
stone building.

The Malindi we saw, however, showed little trace of the splendor and riches of
a once-powerful city-state. And except for a monument commemorating Vasco
de Gama's landing, almost no imprint remained of the two hundred years of Portuguese rule.

When Bob arrived back in Kenya, the children and I got up before dawn and
drove sixty miles down the coast to Mombasa to meet his early morning train.

The road, a sandy track empty of traffic and people, led through sleeping villages and palm groves ghostly in the morning mist. By the time we reached Mombasa the sun was up and the rest of the world awake. I stopped several times to ask directions to the railroad station. The thought of being late and missing Bob began to worry me. What would he do if we weren't there to meet him? Where would he go, and how would I find him? I knew nothing about this busy port of Mombasa and wouldn't have any idea where to go for help. My new found self confidence was slipping.

At the station, when I finally found it, we were just in time to see the train pull in. We watched the long queues of Africans and a few Europeans descend from the train, all of us anxiously scanning each face, but no tall American was among them. Tears stung my eyelids. I felt alone and helpless in this place so far from home. I was about to turn away and try to think what to do next when Bob finally emerged from the door of the last car. Cathy and Robbie raced down the platform and wrapped themselves around him, with Kelly and me close behind. Now we were all crying, tears of joy, sorrow, relief, except Kelly, who was just happy to see her father again.

Bob was physically and emotionally exhausted, and a quiet interlude in Malindi was just what he needed. Our cottage at the Eden Roc Hotel faced the sea. Each day, when the white-robed waiter brought our morning tea at dawn, we drank it on the veranda as the sun rose, red-gold, out of the flat blue Indian Ocean. Cooled and refreshed by an early-morning swim, we were ravenous for a hearty English breakfast, then after a morning in the surf hungry again for lunch, and ready to nap and read until afternoon tea by the pool. There was time for another swim and a walk on the beach before the quick tropical night fell and we returned to our cottage for a bath and a drink before dinner.

The children were required to eat early at the "Children's Dinner," which usually featured something like corn flakes or baked beans on toast. Much to their disgust, they were not permitted in the dining room with us at the eight o'clock "Adult Dinner," though we did manage to smuggle Cathy in a time or two, wearing her most grown-up-looking dress. Most nights we left the three of them under the mosquito nets in our cottage, Kelly snuggling up with Cathy, reading until we returned from the nearby dining room.

Having our Adult Dinners alone gave Bob and me a chance to talk without servants, children, or guests around. Even on the nights in Nairobi when we didn't go out, he often had paper work to finish up in his study while I read in the living room, or took my book to bed. If I asked him, Ali would light a fire in the bedroom before bowing his customary goodnight. I would lie there in its flickering warmth, reading till I fell asleep, or until Bob came and gently removed my book and put out the light.

With this rare opportunity in Malindi for uninterrupted time together, Bob was able to tell me a little about his last visits with his father, though reluctantly, as though the memories were still too painful to share, and about how his mother was coping. He listened sympathetically while I poured out the story of our safari, my fears about doing it and my satisfaction when it was over.

"Good for you!" he said. Then, knowing my notorious lack of mechanical skills, he added, "Lucky you didn't have any car trouble, though!"

During the rest of our stay in Malindi, when I thought about my new sense of accomplishment, it was only as an undercurrent to the familiar rhythm of family life, a sort of hidden melody playing counterpoint to the main theme of my life—my relationship with my husband and children. But hidden though it might be, it was there to stay. I hoped next time we came to Malindi, I wouldn't have to drive those three hundred miles alone. But I knew now that if I had to, I could. Being in Kenya was uncovering some core of independence and strength I hadn't known I had.

This was Kenya's gift to me.

A coastal village near Malindi

Robbie, Kelly, and I on the beach at Malindi

15

AN AMERICAN WITCH DOCTOR?

While we were in Malindi, Joyce's baby was born. I had suggested to Marikus months before that it was time Joyce went home to the family *shamba* in Kisumu, but by then she was pregnant. Marikus asked that she be allowed to stay until the baby was born, and we agreed. He was a big, healthy child whom they named Edward. Joyce carried him on her back as she smoked in the sun, or played with him on the grass near the quarters. She still didn't smile much, nor talk, but I hoped she was happier with a baby to keep her company.

Even Marikus had to admit, though, that his cramped quarters were too small for a family. He went on leave, taking Joyce and the baby back to Kisumu. With him gone, a welcome calm settled over the house in Muthaiga, though it was to be only temporary. Whether I liked it or not, I would be embroiled in Marikus's troubles again. Looking after my extended family, including the often exasperating Marikus, seemed to come with the job of memsahib.

Sometimes that role included playing doctor, as I had with the Kikuyu women. In spite of Nairobi's relatively healthy climate, we and the servants had our share of illnesses. Bob and Robbie had their periodic bouts of gastroenteritis, and Cathy and Kelly suffered through several sieges of tonsillitis. My Asian flu turned out to be a prolonged case, followed by giardia, an intestinal parasite with all the unpleasant symptoms of gastroenteritis and more. Dr. Davies took good care of the children, and Bob and I had found a German doctor who prescribed whatever medications we needed, but I was often the one called on to doctor the servants' ailments—sometimes cuts and bruises, like the Kikuyu women's, but often malaria. Rachel seemed to be immune, but Ali and Marikus, like most other Africans, suffered from recurrent attacks.

The anti-malarial medicine we Americans took, supplied by the Consulate as a preventive, was the same drug used to treat the disease, and the servants knew this. They saw us, and all the Americans we knew, go through the Sunday morning ritual of taking our malaria pills along with our orange juice. If our children spent the night with the Hagbergs or other American friends on a Saturday, or their children stayed with us, we didn't worry. We knew they would all get their malaria pills Sunday morning wherever they were.

So the first time Ali and Marikus became ill with malaria, they asked me for medicine. I checked with our doctor to be sure it was safe, and gave them the prescribed dose. Unfortunately, soon after Marikus returned from Kisumu, another bout struck the two of them just after we had received a new supply of pills. When they came to me, holding their heads and groaning, I counted out their usual number of pills from the new bottle. They took them gratefully and went off to their quarters to lie down.

Later that evening I heard terrible cries and moans coming from the backyard. I ran to the kitchen door and switched on the outside lights. Ali and Marikus were rolling on the grass in agony, retching and clutching their stomachs. Saliva ran from their mouths, and their eyes were glassy. Shocked and frightened, I called Bob. Together we examined the label on the pill bottle.

"Good Lord," Bob said. "These new pills are double the strength of the old ones. You've given them twice their usual dose!"

We had no idea what the effect might be. Panic-stricken, I dialed the King George Hospital and spoke to a British doctor. He was reassuring. Ali and Marikus would probably be very sick for a few hours, he said, but they would not die from an overdose of chloroquin, nor would they suffer any lasting ill effects. I collapsed in the nearest chair and breathed a sigh of relief.

The next morning Ali and Marikus were weary but well: no cramps, no vomiting, no headache, no fever or chills. No malaria! They came to thank me profusely, looking at me with new respect and a certain amount of awe.

"Memsahib dactari mzuri sana," they said. *"Hii dawa kali kabisa!"* (Memsahib is a very good doctor! This medicine is totally strong!") Strong indeed. I had narrowly escaped killing my two patients. Nevertheless, despite my protests, my reputation as an American witch doctor was made. The incident had scared me, though, and after that I lived on my reputation alone. I still doled out bandaids for cuts and aspirin for colds and headaches, but I decided to let Bob take charge of the malaria pills.

Rachel met with her own misfortune one rainy Sunday night. Coming home from her day off, she slipped in the mud behind the quarters and fell, hurting her leg. She dragged herself the rest of the way across slick wet grass to her room and went to bed. All night she lay there in great pain, not wanting to disturb my sleep. In the morning she couldn't walk.

Ali came to fetch me and between us we got her to my car. I took her to Dr. Mwathi, who sent us to the African hospital for an x-ray. While I went to park the car, Rachel was told by an English nurse to get in line and wait. There were no benches, just a long line of Africans standing patiently outside in the hot sun. When I rejoined her, Rachel was leaning against the building, her face gray.

I went to find the nurse and asked that Rachel at least be allowed to sit down inside, as I thought she might have a broken leg. Instantly everything changed. Rachel was no longer just another African. She had a magic talisman: me. She was ushered to the front of the line and taken immediately for her x-ray.

I was at once both relieved and resentful. My white skin had bought help for Rachel, but the rest of the people in line, sick and needing attention, still stood outside with no place to sit, no shelter from the sun. Dogs and horses in Kenya were treated better than this. Fuming, I followed Rachel and the nurse inside.

The x-ray showed that Rachel's leg was indeed broken. At first she refused to have it set and a cast put on. In Swahili she told me of a friend who had had a cast. When it came off the leg was crooked and her friend was a cripple for life. Rachel was fearful of a similar fate. I told her that she was surely going to be a cripple if she didn't allow the doctor to set the shattered bone, and that she would also go on suffering terrible pain. Mentally crossing my fingers, I promised that if the bone were set, it would heal properly and she would not limp. Finally she agreed.

For weeks she hobbled around on crutches with her leg encased in its white cast, still convinced that she would be lame for the rest of her life. To her great joy (and mine), when the cast came off her leg emerged gray-brown, wrinkled, and thin, but straight and strong.

One morning, only a few weeks after Rachel's accident, Bob and I were awakened early by a loud pounding on our bedroom door.

"Bwana, memsahib, there is a woman in Ali's room giving boff!" It was Marikus's voice, high and hysterical. Still groggy with sleep, Bob and I looked at each other, mystified. I reached for my robe. Bob fumbled for his glasses, pulled on a pair of pants, and went to open the door.

"Giving what?" he asked.

"Giving boff! Giving boff!" Marikus repeated urgently. His shirttail was hanging out of his khaki pants, his feet shoved into unlaced sneakers. He appeared excited but not unduly alarmed, almost as though he were enjoying himself. His gaze shifted to me. "She is having baby, memsahib!" he said.

Who's having a baby? I wondered. And why here?

"We'll be right there, Marikus," I said.

Bob and I threw on our clothes and hurried out to the quarters. The girl lay on Ali's bed, not making a sound. She looked very young. Her eyes were wide and frightened. Her hands clutched the bedclothes so tightly the skin over her knuckles looked gray. Ali stood beside her. He bowed politely when I entered.

I looked at him reproachfully. Bob still chuckles at the memory.

"Oh, Ali," I said. "How could you?" How could you bring this pregnant girl here, my thoughts ran, without warning us? How could you let her stay here in labor all night without calling us? Even—totally overlooking the fact that Ali was, after all, a Moslem with no particular commitment to monogamy—how could you get this young girl pregnant when you have a wife and baby in Malindi?

Ali looked perplexed at my question, then replied courteously, "But, memsahib, she is my guest!"

Baffled by this non sequitur, I gave up. Some cultural—and language—gaps can't be bridged.

The drive to the hospital seemed to take forever. The girl's contractions were two minutes apart; her face glistened with sweat and she panted between pains. I had to admire her grit. Though she looked scared to death, only an occasional moan escaped through her clenched teeth. There was no screaming. I squeezed her hand tightly, wondering if I might have to deliver the baby in the back of the car, but Bob got us to the hospital in record time and we handed the girl over to a starchy British matron.

A week or so later Ali brought the girl to see me. She was waiting by the back steps. When I appeared she held out for my inspection a healthy-looking baby boy, black-haired and fair-skinned like many African newborns.

"*Mtoto maradadi sana*," I told her. The baby is very handsome. She ducked her head and smiled but was too shy to answer.

I guessed that on his day off Ali continued to visit the girl and her baby in the African Location where they lived, but he never mentioned them. Not wanting to intrude on his privacy, neither did I. So I never knew what happened to the girl and her baby. I never even knew her name.

16

DIWALI, THE 4TH OF JULY, AND BLOOD PUDDING WITH THE MANGI MKUU

When November came, Rani Khurana invited our family to join their celebration of Diwali, the Festival of Lights, which comes at the time of the October/ November full moon. It marks the Hindu New Year and commemorates the homeward journey, a thousand years before Christ, of the legendary Prince Rama, who had gone to Ceylon to rescue his wife Sita, stolen by a demon. All the way back to India, people lighted their path with *diwa*—little dishes of oil with burning wicks. Every year since, as darkness falls on Diwali, Hindus have placed lighted candles around their houses in memory of Rama's triumphant homecoming

At dusk on Diwali the Parklands section where the Khuranas lived was a magical place, alight with thousands of softly-winking candles that outlined every doorway and walk, every window ledge and flat rooftop, momentarily pricking the darkness with their tiny flames. We helped Rani, Madi and Mahadav set lighted candles along the walk, then sat on the veranda steps to drink in this miracle of light. As the candles burned down and glimmered out, dazzling bursts of fireworks showered across the sky in a Hindu version of a combined Christmas and 4th of July. Later we had one of Rani's incomparable meals, this time a Hindu feast of curry with mounds of fluffy rice, crispy vegetable fritters, stacks of warm *chapattis* for scooping up the curry, and. cucumbers in creamy yogurt to put out the fire.

A few months before this, the Khuranas had joined us in celebrating our own 4th of July, along with nine hundred other invited guests, at Consul General Dudley and Jane Withers' annual reception, their biggest, most gala event of the year. I had been busy for several days, making and freezing several hundred cocktail meatballs as my contribution for the party, and the day before had spent the morning helping to create small corsages of white carnations tied with red and blue ribbon for the American staff wives to wear. I was at the Witherses' all day on the 4th, helping Jane set up tables for the outdoor reception, nailing up bunting, stringing colored lights around the garden.

I went home to change and when I returned, bringing Ali to help, the party was in full swing. People thronged the garden and crowded around tables of food and drinks under blue and white marquees. The American flag fluttered against the blue African sky while from the band came the strains of the Star Spangled Banner. I was struck with amazement to find my eyes filling with tears. Moments of homesickness still struck at unexpected times.

That particular 4th had its tragi-comic side. When someone inadvertently left Dudley's liquor cabinet unlocked, the borrowed servants who had come to help succumbed to the temptation to join the celebration. Unaccustomed to the strong alcohol, they had dropped like flies on the kitchen floor. Ali, a Moslem and a teetotaler, alone had stayed sober. When I went to the kitchen for ice, I found him with sweat pouring down his face, dragging the other servants out the back door onto the grass to sleep it off. At the same time, with his usual cheerful grin, he was doing his best to keep things going in the kitchen.

The following day the children spent all afternoon getting ready for their own 4th of July picnic. They borrowed the red, white, and blue bunting from Jane Withers, dragged all the lawn furniture out of the garage, and dug a barbecue pit. We managed to assemble some typical American food: hot dogs and hamburgers, potato chips and pickles, cokes and the ingredients for s'mores—marshmallows to toast, chocolate bars, and wholemeal biscuits, a British substitute for graham crackers. About sixteen children came, including Mahadav Khurana and the Kianos' son Gaylord, along with several parents. Bob was away in Uganda, so one of the fathers did the barbecuing and another took charge of the fireworks display. Afterward the children ran around the garden, waving sparklers and scattering glittering splinters of light into the night.

I watched them, remembering the 4th of July celebrations in my own childhood, and the ones we and the children had spent with my family at the New Jersey shore. A wave of nostalgia for the familiarity of home was tempered by a warm glow that emanated from the friends around me, from the laughter of the children and the delighted smiles of Ali and Rachel and Marikus, who stood watching with me. Far from home, I was grateful for these American, African, and Asian friends who were my substitute family in Kenya.

We helped celebrate a very different kind of holiday when Bob and I were invited to attend the National Day of the Chaggas, a prosperous tribe who grew coffee on the slopes of Mt. Kilimanjaro in Tanganyika. Bob's secretary stayed at the house with the children, and we made the three-hour trip to the Paramount Chief's elegant white villa in Moshi with several African and Asian friends. If we needed further evidence of Africa's always surprising contrasts, we had it during this trip.

Chief Marealle, whose title was the Mangi Mkuu, was an urbane young man who had been educated in England. His English and manners were perfect. He entertained us in royal style with a display of tribal dancing over which he presided, sitting with regal composure, as though on the finest throne, on a kitchen chair in the courtyard. His polished brown oxfords were planted solidly on a leopard-skin rug, and over his immaculate white shirt and slacks he wore a leopard-skin cape. He held a fly whisk, symbol of authority, in his hand.

The dancing featured a lot of foot stamping, milling around, and pounding on five-foot-long hollowed-out tree trunks. Oddly enough, the dancers performed these traditional Chagga dances in European clothes, the women in cotton dresses and the men in shorts and shirts, shuffling through the motions as though they were bored with the whole thing. It was very different from the tribal dancing we were accustomed to in Kenya, with dancers leaping and twirling in feathers and furs and beads, acting out lion hunts and courtship rituals, and performing intricate gymnastic stunts. In contrast, the Chaggas seemed to be merely paying lip service to a fading tradition.

When the dancing was over, we were invited inside and seated around a long banquet table, where I shortly discovered another tradition, this one still very much alive. We were served a first course of "blood pudding"—a bowl of warm raw blood recently drained from the throat of a sacrificial goat. When it was passed around the table, Bob valiantly took a sip, then handed it to me. Pausing with the bowl in my hands, I felt my stomach quiver and my throat close. Even at the risk of offending our host, I couldn't do it. I passed the bowl quickly to the person next to me. Chief Marealle didn't seem to notice, but I offended him anyway. Following the lead of others at the table, including three young women visiting him from England, I addressed him as Tom. He informed me coolly that in his opinion Americans tend to be much too informal and that he, Chief Marealle, preferred not to advance too quickly to a first-name basis.

Though I tried always to be sensitive to local ways and to avoid violating the customs of the many different cultures we were encountering, this time I had clearly misread the cues. Properly chastened, I was careful after that to call our host Chief Marealle.

Before we left the next day for Nairobi, we drove up the mountain to the Chief's chalet at about eight thousand feet. From the balcony we had a magnificent view of Kilimanjaro's green-carpeted lower flank, covered with the glossy foliage of coffee plantations, and of the dry Tanganyikan plains spreading south beyond Moshi. Behind us towered the peak, an unseen but palpable presence with its snowy head hidden in clouds.

Despite my faux pas, we were added to the Chief's Christmas list that year. When the holiday season came around, one of the more unusual Christmas cards we received was postmarked Moshi and it bore this message: "Season's greetings from the Mangi Mkuu." It was signed Paramount Chief Marealle.

Paramount Chief Tom Marealle

17

AMBOSELI, NGORONGORO CRATER, AND CROSSING THE SERENGETI

We had been in Kenya for ten months before we went on our first big game park safari. Illnesses, Bob's trip to the States when his father died, and the children's school calendar had prevented any long family trips except the one to Malindi. I was eager—we all were—to be out of Nairobi again, out in the bush where we could see more of the country and its always astonishing animals. On a long weekend we packed up for a visit to Amboseli National Park, on Kenya's southern border with Tanganyika.

The main road south from Nairobi was a pleasant surprise—one of the very few outside the city that was paved. Unfortunately, after the turn-off at Namanga, it became like the one I had navigated to Malindi, only worse—a bone-jarring washboard full of ruts and ridges. Breathing choking lungfuls of fine dust, we drove through a parched area of sparse vegetation surrounding a dry lake bed. The miles of scrubby bush flaunted unexpected patches of green wherever an underground spring provided water. High above the hot plain floated the snow-capped peak of Mt. Kilimanjaro, with a layer of clouds wrapped around its shoulders.

At Ol Tukai Lodge, we stayed in two thatched *bandas* where we slept on camp cots, cooked our meals in the kitchen shed out back, and ate on the veranda with a magnificent view of Kilimanjaro. It was an amazing sensation to sit there in shorts, wiping perspiration away, and look up at snowfields atop a mountain that rose dramatically more than nineteen thousand feet out of the plain.

At night there were rustlings in the thatched roof of our *banda*, as little nocturnal creatures went about their secret business under the cover of dark: mice, snakes, lizards, bats, spiders, and a variety of strange insects. As long as they kept their distance and remained hidden in the thatch, I could pretend they weren't there and ignore them. Not so the lions. I lay awake the first night, listening to their grunts and roars echo across the plains, feeling a tingling excitement at what will always be for me the quintessential sound of Africa. I would hear it many times over the years and always my response was the same electric thrill of recognition.

In the morning I went outside in the faint dawn light to watch the rising sun slide above Kilimanjaro's white peak, washing it with pink, then gold. Four lions, loose-limbed and silent, padded by a stone's throw away. I stood motionless, watching, until they disappeared behind some bushes. They had been even closer to camp during the night than I had realized, but they were so completely disinterested in me, and I was so enthralled at seeing them up close, I forgot to be afraid.

Robbie had not been as thrilled as I was with the lions' roars. Rubbing his eyes, he came out of the banda where he had slept with Bob, next to the one I shared with Cathy and Kelly. He and Bob had not gotten much sleep. Bob reported that he had been kept awake most of the night by Robbie's oft-repeated, anxious questions: "Dad! Did you hear that? Was that a lion?" Here, too, his fears haunted him.

During the rains the powdery white surface of Amboseli's dry soda lake sometimes flooded. The lake became, briefly, a shallow pan, attracting large herds of animals and thousands of birds. Vehicles weren't allowed in during the rains, as the roads became impassable, but even during the dry season, when we were there, animals were plentiful. We saw herds of zebra and wildebeest, a family of elephants systematically uprooting a grove of trees and stripping the bark and leaves, a rare gerenuk stretching up on hind legs to reach some tasty foliage. Gertie the Rhino, a long-standing attraction at Amboseli, was easily recognizable by her famous four-foot horn—later broken off in a fight. She was followed by a calf that the game warden told us was famous in its own right, having been born with no visible ears.

Reluctant to leave, we lingered into the afternoon of our last day, watching from the shade of the bandas the maribou storks hunched along the perimeter of camp, the ostriches that occasionally picked their way across the plain, the giraffe that nibbled the top of an acacia tree nearby. It was close to sunset when we finally tore ourselves away and headed back to Nairobi.

On the rough road out of Amboseli we had a flat tire and stopped while Bob changed it. We had passed Namanga and it was almost dusk when we reached the Athi Plain, a barren stretch inhabited mostly by lions and Maasai, and the second tire blew out.

Without a second spare, we sat there, wondering what to do and listening for animal noises as darkness quickly engulfed us. Our drinking water was almost gone, our only remaining food was three oranges. The thought of spending the night here amongst prowling lions, with three tired, hungry children, was daunting.

Luckily, after a half-hour or so, two cars came along and both stopped. People never passed you by in the bush in those days. It was an unwritten rule of the road. In one car was an English family who, it turned out, lived near us in Muthaiga. They took the children and me right to our door.

Meanwhile the man in the other car gave Bob a lift to the nearest village, Athi River. There they found a garage run by a Sikh and some Africans, none of whom spoke English. With the help of his rescuer's Swahili, Bob explained the problem. After infinite delays that involved locating a new tube for the tire, finding a truck, then finding a driver, then finding the key to the petrol pump so they could put petrol in the truck, Bob and two of the African mechanics piled into a truck that had seen better days, and rattled back to our car with the new tube.

Lurching through the blackness, freezing cold in the open cab of the truck, surrounded by unseen wild animals, in the company of two people with whom he could barely communicate, Bob said later he felt as though he were living a bad dream. The sight of our car in the truck's feeble headlights brought him back with a jolt to comforting reality: the everyday problem of a flat tire.

He and his helpers were able at last to get the new tube into the tire. He arrived home late that night, vowing never to go on safari again without two spare tires and a tire-patching kit.

A few weeks later, during the December school holidays, we set out on our longest safari to date. We drove all day, south across the Athi Plain, past Namanga and the road to Amboseli, to the border of Tanganyika and beyond to the west. In the late afternoon, with the jeep's wheels swiveling in sticky black mud from the previous night's rains, we slithered up the mountain road to the rim of Tanganyika's Ngorongoro Crater and on around to Crater Lodge.

The lodge was a cluster of rustic cabins that clung to the very edge of the crater. Fires burned day and night against the chill in this mist-shrouded, mountainous terrain. From our balcony we looked straight down into the crater, where the grass was golden brown in the distant shafts of sunlight, the animals no more than tiny moving dots. We could see the reflected blue of a lake but not the hippos and flamingoes we would see gathered there the next day.

Our cabin was roomy and comfortable, with a tub and hot water in the bath-room and a primitive kitchen where I fixed our simple meals, but no indoor toi-let, no electricity. I had to bring everything we needed with us. The Lodge had a bar where we could have a drink by the fire before dinner, but no meals were served. At night, when we had to use the outhouse a short distance away, we car-ried a lantern and took a good look around, a lesson we learned after an encoun-ter Bob had on our first night. Awakened by a loud snuffling near our door, he pointed his torch outside—full in the face of an enormous buffalo that stood, massive and unmoving, returning his stare. Several times after that, hurrying Kelly through the cold black night, I glimpsed in the bushes the buffalo's long curving horns and mournful eyes as it watched us from behind the outhouse. I was too busy hanging on to the lantern and to Kelly, making sure she didn't fall through the overly large hole in the outhouse, to worry about the buffalo. It seemed peaceful enough anyway, content to remain an observer.

Hyenas lurked around the lodge, too, awaiting their chance to raid the garbage cans. The game warden told us that hyenas had been known to chew through ice chests to get at the food. "They even gnawed the taillights off my car recently," he said, "though I'm at a loss to know why!"

With his warning in mind, we took everything inside the cabin at night and locked up well before we went to bed.

Ngorongoro, the caldera of an extinct volcano, is the largest crater in the world, a huge expanse of green meadow, twelve miles across, enclosed by steep walls two thousand feet high. Our descent the next morning to the crater floor was treacherous, making a four-wheel-drive vehicle a must. A narrow road wound for many miles along the top of the crater to where a muddy track led down. Slip-ping and sliding, we were mired to the hubcaps more than once, even in our jeep. The game warden, who escorted us as far as the crater floor, had to pull us free of the sucking "black cotton" with his Land Rover and chains.

Once down in the crater we left mist and black mud behind. The sun was hot; the animals in their thousands roamed the crater floor. Sunk deep in the earth, Ngorongoro seemed uncannily Biblical and timeless. No roads marred the grassy savannas where the numberless herds grazed. The animals might have been here like this since time immemorial, isolated and protected from the world.

We drove aimlessly for hours, unconfined by roads or boundaries, impelled only by our wonder and curiosity. At one point a pride of eight lions paced ner-vously around our jeep. I circled them slowly so Bob could take pictures. Cathy and Robbie's voices, sounding anxious, came from the back seat:

"Mo—ther, come on, let's go!" I was getting too close for comfort, apparently. But not for Kelly. "Nice kitty," she crooned to one big male. "Does he speak English, Mama?" It was a question she frequently asked about people. Why not lions?

On the next breath she commanded, "Let's get out for lunch!"

Laughter filled the car when Bob asked, "Whose lunch?"

We drove on among the whitened skulls, horns, and bones that littered the ground, remnants of kills by Ngorongoro's predators. A horde of vultures fed on a carcass; farther along a hyena dragged away the leg of an animal. On a gentle slope several rhinos grazed, rows of tickbirds perched on their backs. A mother with a calf eyed us suspiciously as we came near, then warned us off with angry stampings and head shakings.

A cloud of dust heralded the sudden movement of a giant herd of zebra, kongoni, and wildebeest that thundered across our path. We waited what seemed a long time before the last of them passed by on their unknown mission to somewhere. They may have been startled into flight by a predator, but we saw none. Only a lone hyena that skulked away as the dust cleared, and two bat-eared foxes that stretched on their hind legs to stare before turning to run.

We were back up at the lodge by dusk, leaving behind the sunlit crater floor with its broad open reaches and great herds, like a mystical memory of the earth as it was in the dim dawn of prehistory.

Our homeward safari by a different route, across the Serengeti Plain to Kenya, did nothing to dispel our feeling of having slipped into a time warp. I wonder now that we had the courage—or foolhardiness—to make such a trip. Bob had gotten a pass that permitted us to travel through an area ordinarily closed to Europeans, since it was wild and uninhabited except for animals and a few Maasai. As I still occasionally did, I hung back, weighing the dangers, but Bob was raring to go. He took the precaution of giving the game warden at Ngorongoro our planned route and time schedule. The warden promised to alert his counterpart at Narok, in Kenya, and assured us that if we failed to turn up by nightfall, an immediate search would be mounted. Car trouble represented the greatest threat, since it would leave us stranded and unprotected, if night came, from predators like lions.

On the Serengeti we couldn't count on passing vehicles to help us, as they had on our Amboseli safari. We carried our own gas, food, and water, as well as the usual spare parts, two tires, and the tire-patching kit. Thus prepared, and lulled by the sense of security provided by the game warden, we set out.

From the rim of Ngorongoro Crater the road swept down through green hills until we reached the Serengeti. Endless brown grasslands stretched to the horizon. Only the distant mountains to the east broke the flat rim of the world. Animals galloped away at our approach, to melt into invisibility as they were swallowed by billows of red dust.

The road was barely a road at all. We spent a good bit of time just looking for it. More than once it disappeared completely. In some places thousands of hoof marks obliterated the two tire-tracks; in others the road's deep ruts became muddled in a network of game and cattle trails that led off in a dozen directions. The faraway range of mountains in the east provided the only landmark to keep us heading north.

Near the southern edge of the Serengeti we passed Olduvai Gorge, site of another of the Leakeys' famous digs. No one was working there at the time, but Bob walked a short way up the gorge for a look while I stayed in the jeep with the children. A desolate moonscape of bleached layers of earth rose on either side of him, each layer a slice representing millions of years.

"It was like walking back through the millennia to a time before man existed," he said later. "There was no sign that anyone had ever been there before me, and no sound but the whirring and humming of insects. I kept thinking that each twist of the gorge could bring me face to face with…something. I didn't know what. It was so eerie, it made the hair stand up on the back of my neck."

After a few hundred feet he turned and, keeping a sharp lookout for snakes and scorpions, hurried to retrace his steps. He saw nothing, heard nothing as he walked through the great empty silence until he came within sight of the jeep and our reassuring human presence. I had been waiting tensely and breathed a sigh of relief when he emerged through shimmers of dusty sunlight from the hidden recesses of the gorge.

At lunchtime we picnicked under a thorn tree in the middle of the plain. All day we saw no other cars, nor any people save for a few Maasai with their herds in the distance. We passed through no towns or villages, nor was there any place to buy petrol. There were just the animals, the birds, the heat and the dust, and us. We counted twenty-five species of game that day and an unknown number of birds: crowned cranes, loftily patrician with black and white feathers touched with splashes of violet, vermilion, and gold; awkward-looking secretary birds with ragged head feathers and quill-like tails; brilliant little sun birds, like scraps of scarlet, indigo, and emerald that darted from the bushes; storks, bustards, vultures, and many more that we couldn't identify.

Late in the afternoon, near the northern edge of the plain, we came to a tiny settlement. At a little Indian duka beside the road, Maasai women were wrangling with each other and bargaining with the shop owner over coils of silver and copper wire. Their goatskin dresses and cloaks were covered with elaborate beadwork and they wore many ornaments of wire and beads. Most had babies strapped to their backs. We welcomed the sight of other people, after our solitary day on the plain, but the women didn't answer our greetings or return our smiles, or even look at us, but just went on quarreling among themselves.

At dusk we reached Narok, a collection of small dukas, police station, and game warden's post, and checked in with the warden. Great was our surprise and disillusionment when we found that our arrival was totally unexpected. Word of our Serengeti crossing had failed to reach Narok. Had we had any trouble—car or otherwise—help would have been a long time coming, if it ever did.

We got back to Nairobi about nine-thirty that night, the jeep and ourselves covered in layers of caked mud and dust. Marikus and Ali had kept a hot dinner waiting. As so often, I was once again grateful, not only for their help, but for their willingness to adapt so good-naturedly to our sometimes unpredictable comings and goings. I fell asleep that night feeling as though I had been on a long, long journey through time, a journey of far more than just a few days.

18

KINYONA: A VISIT WITH SENIOR CHIEF NJIIRI

The week after Christmas, Kariuki invited us to visit his father, Senior Chief Nji-iri, in Kinyona. With Kariuki and Ruth, the Kianos, and all our children, we traveled in a caravan of cars, stopping along the way to visit some of Kariuki's brothers who were chiefs, like their father. At each village we were mobbed by friendly people wanting to shake our hands and greet us. Kariuki returned the greetings by handing out holiday gifts of pencils and hard candies to all the children.

At Chief Ndungu's we had morning tea; and at Chief Kigo's a hearty lunch of the inevitable roast goat, Kikuyu sausage, and vegetables fresh from the farm. Chief Kigo had five wives, he told us proudly, and they had produced many children. One wife was at that very moment in the hospital in labor, another just home with a new baby, and a third far advanced in pregnancy. Laughing heartily, the chief confided that he had to work very hard to keep all his wives happy. He said, however, that they got along well, that they cooked together, worked in each other's shambas, and helped care for each other's children. Though many modern women in Kenya today feel differently, the four wives we met at Chief Kigo's acted more like sisters than rivals and seemed truly lacking in the kind of jealousy that Westerners might feel.

I had been reading Jomo Kenyatta's book, *Facing Mount Kenya*, in which he explained why polygamy worked for the Kikuyu. Kikuyu male children, he said, were brought up to "cultivate the idea and technique of extending their love to several women" while "girls are taught to share a husband's love."

In order to avoid jealousy, he continued, custom provided that "each wife must be visited by her husband on certain days of the moon...and the wives see to it that the husband does not neglect his duty."

Chief Kigo had clearly not been neglecting his duty.

At teatime we reached Senior Chief Njiiri's compound, tidy rows of thatched huts on a meadow of thick green grass. Set on a hillside in the heart of Kikuyuland, sixty miles from Nairobi, it looked out over ranks of dark green ridges toward the dim blue Aberdare Mountains to the west and the jagged black peak and glistening snow of Mt.Kenya in the east. The smoky air held a damp, high-altitude chill. I shivered and pulled my sweater more closely around me.

Senior Chief Njiiri came to greet us. He was an imposing figure in his monkey fur cape and a red beret spangled with medals from the King and Queen of England, with more medals marching across his chest. His face was craggy and deeply lined, like ancient African teak, and under black brows his eyes were heavy-lidded, his mouth stern until he smiled. In a mixture of Swahili, Kikuyu, and English he chatted with us about the weather, the view, our health and our families. Kariuki translated when necessary.

According to Kariuki, his father had thirty-some wives, each with her own round mud-and-wattle hut. We walked between the huts along neatly swept paths to the *thingira*—the men's house and meeting hall, an oblong structure with a corrugated tin roof into which the men disappeared. Women and girls were not allowed inside; instead we visited the home of Kariuki's mother, the senior wife.

I had to bend over to squeeze through the open doorway. Inside, I stopped to let my eyes adjust to the dark smokiness. In the center of the hard-packed dirt floor I could dimly make out a fire surrounded by three cooking stones. Alcoves around the outer wall were separated by partitions and contained benches where the mother and daughters slept on beds of straw. Two of the alcoves held firewood and cooking utensils; others were used as pens where the sheep and goats were kept at night. Sons were sent at an early age to a special boys' house until they could join the men in the *thingira*.

We squatted on beaded, three-legged wooden stools around the fire while the Chief's wife showed us how she balanced her cooking pot on the three stones to make her porridges and stews. She offered us Kikuyu beer, smiling and nodding her shaved head encouragingly, her enormous beaded earrings swinging and clanking. The beer was passed around in a buck's horn from which each of us took a swig. With a deep breath and a prayer that the alcohol had killed all the germs, I swallowed a mouthful. It was honey-smooth and quite delicious.

By now Kariuki had joined us, so I asked how his mother prepared the beer. It was brewed in a big calabash, he said, from a mixture of honey, sugar cane, and a fermenting agent. The outside of the calabash was rubbed with goat's dung for insulation, and then it was set on a hot stone by the fire. In twenty-four hours the beer was ready to drink.

Eyes still smarting from the smoke, we made our way back to the Chief's big stone house, which he used for entertaining only, preferring to live in his traditional thatched hut. Outside, in a grassy clearing, we were given a demonstration of grinding millet for porridge. Four of the wives, clad in blankets over goatskins, with the now-familiar shaved heads and hoops of beads, stood around a hollowed-out tree trunk set upright on the ground. Each holding a long club with a knob on one end, they rhythmically pounded the grain in turn, first one, then the next, and so on round and round until the millet was like fine flour. At the women's urging, Ruth and Ernestine and I took a turn, but we were hopelessly inept. Our arms lacked the strength for pounding and we couldn't get the rhythm right. The women cackled delightedly at our feeble attempts.

The Chief invited the adults—men and American women only—to come into his stone house for "tea." I groaned inwardly. More food! I felt stuffed like a fat Kikuyu sausage already. We were served goat stew again, and heaps of rice and vegetables, by some of the wives, who then ate separately according to custom.

Tea was followed by speeches and gifts. Chief Njiiri spoke first. In Kikuyu he welcomed us, his son's American friends, and then described his vision of a future world that awaited us. One day, he predicted, we would no longer think of ourselves as Americans, Europeans, or Kikuyu, black or white, but would all be one people. When that time came, he said, wars would end.

It was a poignant hope, freighted with the terrible, still fresh memories of Mau Mau. I closed my eyes and wished that this utopian dream might come true. For a moment, it seemed almost possible.

Chief Njiiri then called upon "Mr. Robert" to say a few words.

The Kikuyu love to give people nicknames. Bob's, bestowed by Kikuyu friends in Nairobi, was Mwenda Andu, Lover of People. The Lover of People thanked the Chief for entertaining us and told him how much we had enjoyed meeting Kariuki's family, and then Chief Njiiri announced that "She Who Has Many Children And May She Double The Number" would speak next.

He meant me! When I became pregnant with our fourth child the following year, I wondered if I were destined, whether I liked it or not, to live out this Kikuyu wish/blessing.

I too thanked the Chief for the warm hospitality we had been shown, and he responded by presenting me with a live goat. When I explained that I hadn't enough land to keep a goat, he graciously gave me instead a goat leg to roast, and baskets of bananas and cabbages.

Meanwhile the children were outside where some of the wives and daughters had organized a Kikuyu dance. We came out to find Cathy in the circle, swaying and shaking her hips. Kelly was being handed around among the remaining wives, who were admiring her red plaid dress and fingering her blond curls. Although she usually objected to this kind of familiarity from strangers, she was taking it all in stride.

Chief Njiiri would live on for a number of years. Kariuki never knew his father's exact age, but when the old Chief died in 1978 he was believed to be about ninety. He lived long enough to see his country become independent and his son and some of his fellow tribesmen take over the leadership of the new government of Kenya.

Senior Chief Njiiri

Kelly and I walk through Chief Njiiri's village.

From left, Kariuki, Cathy, Gikonyo Kiano, and Bob pounding millet

Kariuki's mother, his father, Chief Njiiri, Kariuki Njiiri with son Kari, and Ruth Njiiri. Two of the Chief's extended family in the background

Dr. Gikonyo Kiano and Chief Njiiri. Robbie and Gaylord Kiano on the steps,
Kariuki Njiiri in the background, left

19

COOKING AT THE Y

At the December Board meeting of the YWCA, I was asked if I would be willing to teach cooking to a class of African girls. I had been serving on the Board for several months, attending the monthly meetings and occasionally helping to hostess a luncheon or tea. The cooking class would be part of an effort being undertaken by the YWCA to educate African girls. By 1958 there were many who had completed the 8th grade and passed the Kenya African Preliminary Exam (KAPE), which qualified them for entrance into high school or a teacher training college. Unfortunately, there were far too few schools for them to attend. Instead, most of them would return to their villages, with no hope of further education.

To address the problem, the Y Board established the first program of vocational education for girls in Kenya. Funds were raised for a building to house the girls, and in January 1959, the first class of twelve arrived. They came from all over Kenya, some from remote areas where they had never imagined refrigerators or electric lights, never climbed a staircase or used a flush toilet. They settled in amazingly quickly, and classes began. The girls received practical training by assisting with catering, cooking, cleaning and laundry at the Y, and qualified volunteers were recruited to teach them English, child care, first aid, home nursing, cooking, nutrition and hygiene.

When Edna Collins, the Scotswoman who directed it, explained the program, she stressed that the goal was not to train the girls to be domestic servants. Instead, they would be offered a broad curriculum that after two years would enable them to take further exams and go on to a wide variety of occupations. In addition, they would learn to mix freely with Europeans, become better wives and mothers, and help create an African middle class. These were goals that I was all in favor of, and I wanted to help. I had been trained as a teacher, and I had been cooking for my family for quite a few years. So without quite knowing what I was getting into, I had volunteered.

I met the girls once a week in the Y's big kitchen, where we spent Tuesday afternoons concocting dishes that could be served in the dining hall at the Y hostel. The girls, plunged into strange surroundings, far from their homes, were shy but cooperative. They arrived in the kitchen wearing clean white aprons over their YWCA school uniforms, their faces eager They listened carefully to my explanations of recipes and watched my demonstrations closely. We ended the lessons with the girls copying the day's recipe in their notebooks in English.

With a limited budget, I used local foodstuffs that were plentiful and cheap, and recipes of my own or Betty Crocker's that I hoped would appeal to local tastes. The first week we made banana bread, bananas being a familiar part of most Kenyans' diets and readily available. There is also not much you can do to ruin banana bread, so it seemed a safe choice. I had the altitude to contend with of course, but fortunately my Betty Crocker cookbook had high altitude adjustments for most recipes.

With *posho* we baked cornbread and corn muffins, and with minced steak—one of the cheaper meats in Nairobi—made meat loaf and chili, substituting Kikuyu beans for kidney beans and adding a few hot peppers from the Indian bazaar. The girls made their first Boston baked beans and potato salad, and learned to bake scones and cookies. I also had to include that favorite British dessert, pudding. Custards were easy, but it was when I tried to corral the ingredients for old-fashioned cornstarch pudding that I ran into the confusion over cornstarch and corn flour and Taj Nanji at the Nairobi Provisions Store had to straighten me out.

A few weeks into the course, Miss Collins asked me if I would teach the girls to stuff and cook an ox heart the following week. She ordered it from the butcher shop, and when I arrived it lay there on the table, waiting for me, rubbery, dark purply-red, and unappetizing—a part of the ox's anatomy I had never had any desire to either cook or eat, and still don't. The girls stood behind the tables in their white aprons, also waiting expectantly.

Reading straight out of *The Kenya Settlers' Cookery Book*, I showed them how to wash the heart well, cram it with bread stuffing, tie it, brown it, and let it simmer three hours until tender. The girls reported the following week that it tasted "very nice," and they planned to cook it again soon. I was happy to take their word for it. In fact, they always said, if I asked, that the food we prepared was "very nice." I never knew for sure if they were just being polite or really liked the various American dishes I introduced them to. At least the ingredients were almost always familiar, though often combined in different ways.

The Kenya Settlers' Cookery Book, published in 1928, had turned up in the kitchen cupboard of our house in Muthaiga. No one else claimed it so I appropriated it. I have it still. It is full of handy hints for the settler housewife—not just recipes but safari lists, directions for soap-making, notes on raising poultry (including care of a "broody hen"), home remedies for Nairobi fly and ringworm, and orders to servants in Swahili and Kikuyu. Other recipes besides the stuffed ox heart make interesting reading. Five pages of mealie (maize) recipes run the gamut from Mealie Green Soup to Mealie Pie. The directions for something called Brawn start out with "cleaning, blanching, and boiling sheep's trotters (feet??) until tender;" and in a recipe for Scottish Haggis, the cook is instructed to boil the bag (stomach) and the pluck (heart, lungs, liver and windpipe) for two hours, letting the windpipe hang out of the pot.

It's a cookery book that could easily spoil your appetite. The ox heart recipe was the only one I ever had the courage to try.

The coal stove we cooked on was a temperamental black behemoth. Usually someone on the staff lit it before I arrived, but one week whoever it was forgot. The girls and I did our best, but an hour and a half later the stove was still cold. When I left, the biscuit dough we had mixed was in the refrigerator and the girls were still struggling with the stove.

Teaching cooking with a stove that sometimes refused to light, using a "cookery" book full of unfamiliar terms, and trying to shop for ingredients whose names were a mystery sometimes lent an air of absurdity (not to mention a familiar tinge of African-style frustration) to the whole venture. I marveled that we had any successes at all. I've also sometimes wondered in the years since how many of the recipes in the notebooks survived, and how many families in Kenya are eating American-style meat loaf, chili, and cornbread as a result of those cooking classes at the Y.

Even after several weeks the girls, like the other Kenyan women I knew, remained shy. They listened politely when I tried to start a conversation about something other than cooking, but my questions were answered with monosyllables and the girls seldom volunteered anything. They were soon serving tea and homemade cookies to guests at the Y and even putting on luncheons for distinguished visitors. When I appeared each week they proudly reported these accomplishments. But most of the time I still couldn't get them to open up very much and talk to me.

Then one day, while we were washing up after a lesson, I happened to mention that I had been to the Game Park the day before. "I still get excited when I see lions," I said. "That's something I guess I'll never get accustomed to!"

The kitchen went still. Twelve pairs of hands paused in the soapy water, twelve pairs of dark eyes looked at me from all parts of the room. Esther broke the silence.

"I have never seen a lion, Madam." (I hadn't been able to break them of this mission-ingrained habit and get them to call me by name.) "I do not think any of us have." Eleven heads nodded agreement.

It was my turn to register shock. How could they have lived all their lives in Africa and never seen lions? I realized, upon reflection, that this is probably true of many Africans; they are surrounded by wildlife they never see. The animals generally avoid the villages, especially in daylight, and at night when the big game hunts, feeds, and drinks at the water holes, the villagers are safe in their houses. I remembered how thrilled Ali and Rachel were when we took them to the Game Park. They had never seen lions or giraffes or most of the other animals either.

I went to see Edna Collins. "Could I take the girls on an outing to the Game Park?" I asked. "They say they've never seen lions!"

Her face lighted up with a warm smile. "I don't see why not. Yes! What a lovely experience for them. Thank you for suggesting it!"

Excitement broke their customary reserve when I told them. A babel of Swahili/Luo/Kikuyu filled the kitchen. They could hardly wait for the day to come.

Miss Collins offered to go along, as we needed two cars. With our cargo of giggling teenagers, released from the familiar confines of the Y, we set out the following week on our great adventure. Almost at once we found a pride of lions sprawled in the short grass, and parked beside them on the plain. The girls were fascinated but nervous about being so close, though we reassured them that most animals will not attack a vehicle, and as long as we stayed in the cars we were safe.

At the hippo pool we stopped for a picnic. The snouts and giant nostrils of several submerged "river horses" broke the calm surface. The girls looked around warily as they ate, shivering at the sign nailed to a tree: "Beware of Crocodiles."

Just as we got back in the cars, a troop of baboons arrived and climbed all over our vehicles. We warned the girls not to open the windows, baboons being notorious for reaching inside cars and grabbing anything edible, or even anything portable.

Driving slowly along after our picnic, we followed the rutted tracks that meandered through herds of gazelles and zebras. A family of wart hogs trooped single file through the long grass, short tails straight up and vibrating like small antennae. Ostriches sprinted away with stiff giant steps; giraffes browsed on the flat tops of acacia trees. The girls giggled and nudged each other, pointing at animals and asking me their names in English and Swahili. The sun had dropped into heavy gray clouds by the time we drove out of the park. It was dark when we delivered the girls back to the Y.

A few days later I received a thank-you note signed by several of the girls. In neat handwriting and polished English, the girls thanked me for taking them to the Game Park where they "saw very many animals which we had only read about in stories, but which we had never seen, especially the lions."

Toward the end of the year, shortly before we were leaving for the States, I invited the girls and Miss Collins to a farewell tea at my home. It was a somewhat rare event—a group of African girls being entertained in Muthaiga in broad daylight. When African friends did come to our house in the evening for dinner, we tried not to flaunt their presence. They came either in mixed groups of whites, blacks, and Asians, often for a semi-official function such as Dr. Mwathi's party, or one or two couples came alone. This was partly for their sakes, but also for our own. We wanted neither to get them into trouble nor ourselves ejected from Kenya for "fraternizing" with Africans, which was clearly frowned on.

Throughout our two years in Kenya, there was always this underlying tension around our friendships with Africans. General Sir George Erskine, the commander of the British forces in East Africa, lived just down the street, and the barracks of the Kings' African Rifles were at the end of Muthaiga Road, a couple of miles away. Bob and I felt eyes always upon us, watching, judging, condemning, our activities probably being reported. The State Department even sent a security officer up from South Africa to check our phones and make sure they weren't bugged.

I hoped that my African students would be looked upon differently. Surely inviting some young girls to tea could not be seen as threatening or subversive.

Marikus for some reason seemed reluctant to help with the preparations. I sensed disapproval but I didn't know why. It couldn't be because the girls were Africans. He was always delighted when we entertained African friends like Tom Mboya or Gikonyo Kiano. The minute he and Ali heard Tom and Gikonyo's voices they would appear in the living room, faces stretched wide with welcoming grins, eager to shake hands. As usual, I couldn't fathom the depths of Marikus's mind. Did he object to the extra work? But Marikus never complained about extra hours in the kitchen. It was his realm, the place where in my absence he ruled, the place where he excelled. Was it because, unlike Tom and Gikonyo, these girls were not prominent African leaders with faces and names well-known throughout Kenya? Was it because they were girls? I would never know.

I resorted to an appeal to his vanity. "Let's show my students what a really lovely tea you can lay on, Marikus!" I said.

He responded by outdoing himself, preparing trays of tiny sandwiches and helping me bake cookies and brownies. He even assisted Ali in serving so that he would have an excuse to come into the living room to receive the class's compliments.

The girls came in their best dresses and Sunday shoes, drank tea, ate cookies and sandwiches, and sat talking with Miss Collins and me, then we strolled around the garden and down to the river. I wondered if some of my white neighbors were having fits. Well, let them, I thought.

I would learn later from a friend on the Y Board that when the girls finished their two years of training, all twelve passed their final examinations with high marks, and all found jobs. Lilian and Leah were invited to accompany Sir Michael Wood of the Flying Doctor Service to Tanganyika to teach Child Care to village women, and later did similar village work in Kenya. Esther became a YWCA Warden and won a scholarship to Bath Domestic Science College in England. The others became receptionists, caterers, village Y Club leaders, matrons at local colleges and YWCA hostels. The Y program would continue for a number of years, filling an important niche in the education of Kenyan women and preparing many of them for the new roles they would fill in independent Kenya.

On the day of the tea, I was impressed with how far the girls had come in a little less than a year, how much they had gained in self-assurance and poise. The painfully shy girls and the giggling teenagers had vanished. These were young women, ready for the new Kenya.

The Girls in the YWCA Cooking Class

Elisheba Mbidiku	Lilian Njeri
Leah Wangeri	Betha Masidza
Beth Njhira	Esther Wairumu
Agnes Olesia	Paula Olesia
Edith Wanjiru	Esther Bugutsa
Bilha Masida	Violet Wanjiru

20

THE QUEEN MOTHER COMES TO VISIT

One day in January, the mail Bob brought home at lunchtime included an engraved invitation, bearing a royal golden seal. It said:

To have the honour of meeting
Her Majesty Queen Elizabeth The Queen Mother
His Excellency the Governor
and
The Lady Mary Baring
request the pleasure of your company
at a Garden Party to be held at Government House Nairobi
on Saturday, 7th February, 1959 at 3:30 P.M.

Sometimes I felt as though I had stumbled into someone else's life. Who was this woman who had been invited to Government House to meet the Queen Mother? She didn't seem like someone I knew. The memories of the years in the drafty student housing at Willow Run, of counting up prices at the grocery store lest they exceed the twenty dollars in my wallet for food each week, were still too fresh in my mind. If I had imagined my future then, I would have pictured life in a university town as the wife of a college professor, living on a modest income. Before that, when I was growing up, I had hoped that I wouldn't spend my life in my own hometown in suburbia, but would live in a more glamorous place. New York, for instance, safely nearby but exciting, or some other big city not too far away. Living in Africa and meeting the Queen Mother of England were never part of that scenario.

Unlikely as it seemed, though, the names on the invitation were ours, and I was soon caught up in the excitement over the Queen Mother's visit. The whole country came down with an acute attack of royal mania. In Nairobi roads were resurfaced and lined with pots of flowers, huge gilt crowns were hung down the length of Delamere Avenue, buildings were decorated with bunting, and flags flew everywhere.

Although some of their leaders were not so enthusiastic about the Queen Mother's visit, most Africans prepared to welcome Mama Mzee (Old Mother) like the most loyal of Britons. Inexplicably, their resentment of British rule did not seem to extend to the Royal Family, who were venerated as the ultimate tribal leaders. Like other colonized peoples, Kenya Africans had internalized some of the values, attitudes, and traits of the very people they rebelled against—their accents, their dress, their educational goals, their religion, and their passion for the Royal Family. The pageantry may have been partly what appealed to them, the bunting and bands and air of festivity reminders of the days of the great *ngomas*, when the tribes gathered together in their lionskins, colobus furs, feathers and beads, to dance their traditional dances.

The day Queen Mother Elizabeth arrived, I took my Girl Guide Company to join the throngs of Africans, Asians, and Europeans who lined the streets of Nairobi, cheering, waving flags, and tossing flowers. The Queen Mother passed down Government Road in her open car, smiling and nodding and waving, only an arm's length away. Blue-eyed and youthful-looking, she had the famous English peaches-and-cream complexion, but what I remember most clearly was her smile: warm and gracious, but disconcertingly marred by teeth stained a tea-color brown.

Included with the invitation Bob and I received from the Governor and Mrs. Baring were instructions about parking and a directive about appropriate attire: long white gloves and hats for the ladies, morning suits and homburgs for the men. I got out the little black hat I had worn on the plane coming to Kenya, and Bob brushed off a dark business suit, the closest thing he had to striped pants and a morning coat. I borrowed long gloves and he borrowed a homburg, which he had to stuff with Kleenex to keep it from falling down over his eyes.

On the day of the garden party Nairobi produced one of its sparkling days: brilliant in the sun, deliciously cool in the shade. Cathy, in her blue Girl Guide uniform, went with us to help serve tea in the tea tent. Narrow skirts were in fashion that year, and my coral linen dress, produced by a local tailor, was high style. I was also wearing the kind of shoes we tortured ourselves with back then: black pumps with cruelly pointed toes and stiletto heels. Hobble-skirted and teetering, I maneuvered my way through an awkward curtsy as the Queen Mother made her ceremonial tour among the crowd. She was "radiant in blue, which reflected the color of her eyes," as the press was fond of saying. After her stroll around the garden she sat on the terrace for the rest of the afternoon, drinking tea and watching the band of the King's African Rifles as it played and paraded. Flags flew in the light breeze, ladies in summer dresses moved about on the green lawn among colorful beds of flowers, and the Queen Mother chatted and nodded charmingly to all.

I felt as though I had been transported to another century, dropped into a story by Kipling. We were all actors, playing our parts. *Rule Britannia!* in living color. In a moment the Bengal lancers would appear over the brow of the hill, waving the British flag and pursuing a horde of barbarians.

"Come out of your trance and drink your tea!" said Bob, handing me a steaming cup.

The illusion vanished. I was back in Africa, back in my own century. But the scene before me remained, a dreamlike image of a colonial life that was already over. At six o'clock the band beat retreat. The Queen Mother left and we were allowed to leave too. The party was over.

The following day Kelly, after hearing all the talk, requested in the English accent she was acquiring that she be taken to see the "Queen Mothah," so we walked to the end of Karura Avenue and watched Her Majesty go by in a car on her way to church. Her schedule and route were printed in the paper every day so people would know where to watch for her. Twice while she was in Nairobi I got stuck in town, as all traffic was stopped for a half-hour before she was due. Snarled traffic and choked sidewalks became a way of life during her visit, and when the papers reported that "thousands lined the streets," it was no exaggeration. We had no choice.

During her visit, the Queen Mother officially opened the Aberdare National Park, crossing the wild remote mountains on the newly improved road and picnicking beside a waterfall. The Aberdares had been closed to the public throughout the Mau Mau Emergency, when bands of rebels had taken refuge there in the dense bamboo forests and high empty moors. After the Queen's visit, when the road was opened to the public, we were part of the first private party to travel across it.

I had been looking at the distant outline of these mountains for some months, whenever we were outside Nairobi, or high up in the Ngong Hills from where they were visible. They looked mysterious and forbidding, especially when I remembered Hassan Rattansi's tales of his parents' arduous journeys across them and the frightening stories about Mau Mau. But I was intrigued at the thought of seeing them up close, and if it was safe for the Queen Mother, then it was no doubt safe for us too.

We arrived at the Outspan Hotel in Nyeri, on the edge of the Aberdares, in the early afternoon. After a rest, we attended the wedding reception of Ann and Duncan Ndegwa, friends we had met in Nairobi. Ann had graduated from high school and from one of the few teacher-training colleges for African women. Duncan was a recent graduate of the University of Edinburgh, one of the small minority of African men who were educated in Britain. He went on to have a distinguished career as advisor to President Kenyatta and as Governor of the Central Bank of Kenya. He and Ann had been married that morning at the church in their hometown of Nyeri, and we arrived in time for the reception.

Dozens of Ann's and Duncan's relatives and friends crowded the grassy compound in front of the church. The celebration was a blend of Kikuyu and European customs: Ann wore a white wedding gown and was attended by four bridesmaids in pink, but most of the other women guests wore the traditional goatskins and kangas. Duncan's dark suit and tie contrasted with the assortment of raincoats, khaki shorts, sweaters, and surplus army overcoats on many of the men. And in the center of a long outdoor table a tiered, white-frosted wedding cake was flanked by platters of roasted goat and bowls of sweet potatoes and *irio*, a Kikuyu favorite that I was quite fond of too. It looks like green mashed potatoes, and in fact is a tasty mixture of peas, beans, and sometimes other vegetables, cooked and mashed with potatoes. One of Ann's friends brought cups of tea to me and the children, but Bob joined the men drinking *njohi*—honey beer—from a gourd.

That evening, after dinner at the Outspan, we put the children to bed and adjourned to the bar, where local settlers were playing darts, drinking ale, and exchanging farm talk and local gossip. We were joined for drinks by Billy Woodley, Game Warden for the Aberdares and a former Mau Mau fighter, who had spent the past few years hunting down terrorists in the mountains. When he heard we were planning to cross the Aberdares the next day, he offered to be our guide. He had a reassuring air of competence and I was glad he was coming along.

The weather stayed bright and clear as we set off behind Billy's jeep the next morning. The road wound upward through large Kikuyu villages that gave way after a while to thick forest. The air cooled rapidly as we climbed. Billy, blond, sun-tanned, trim in his khaki uniform, stopped his jeep several times to point out the camp sites of notorious Mau Mau leaders and of those who fought against them. The camps were deserted now, already overgrown and reverting to forest.

The only signs of life were the troops of long-haired colobus monkeys leaping about in the treetops, flashes of black and white in the gloom.

Above eight thousand feet the forest ended, replaced by a belt of bamboo. The thin hollow trunks formed a solid wall on either side of the road, rattling and moaning eerily in the wind. Narrow paths trampled by elephants and rhino laced the seemingly impenetrable mass. Mau Mau fighters on both sides had used these trails, Billy said, "but it was a risky business. If you met an elephant or rhino face to face, there was no escape except to turn around and run—FAST!"

Late in the morning we emerged from the greenish twilight of the bamboo onto open moorlands as wild and rugged as any in Scotland. At eleven thousand feet, we were above the tree line. The moors rolled away, cold and empty except for outcroppings of rocks and strange-looking plant forms, including grotesquely shaped giant lobelias towering over our heads. At this altitude, even in brilliant sunshine, we were glad of our heavy sweaters and jackets. At night the temperature sometimes dropped below freezing and the moors were white with frost. I thought with a pang of Hassan Rattansi's little sister, crossing these unforgiving mountains with her parents, forty years before, and dying of hypothermia here.

We had a picnic lunch in a sheltered spot behind some rocks, interrupted only once when someone yelled, "Rhino!" and we all dashed off to watch it grazing quietly on the opposite hillside. Later Billy, who had accompanied the Queen Mother on her crossing of the Aberdares, showed us the waterfall where she had her picnic in a banda constructed especially for the occasion. He had been quite smitten with Her Majesty.

"A lovely lady," he said. "And ah, those beautiful blue eyes!"

At sunset we came to the highest point on the road and stopped to look in awe at what seemed to be half of Kenya. At our feet the mountain fell away to the Kinangop plateau, then dropped again to the floor of the Rift Valley over a mile below. Across the Rift, beyond Lake Naivasha shining like a piece of dull silver, beyond the volcanic cones of Longonot and Suswa, rose the far escarpment, forty miles distant. In the sunset light the Rift floor and the mountains glowed with desert hues of mauve and rose and midnight blue, shifting and fading as we watched.

We descended to the floor of the Rift and in another of those disorienting leaps through time and space that happened to me often in Kenya, were back home in Nairobi that night.

Ann and Duncan Ndegwa on their wedding day

Our caravan entering the Aberdare National Park. Game Warden Billy Woodley
and guard

Waterfall in the Aberdare Mountains

Picnic in the Aberdares—Cathy, Robbie, Game Warden Billy Woodley and friend

21

ELEPHANT COUNTRY

The children's final school term in September 1959 had already begun when Bob found that he had to make another trip to Uganda. This time we decided to take the children out of school and go with him. Our time in Kenya was becoming precious. There wouldn't be many more long safaris. When Bob's USIS business was completed in Kampala, we would go on to visit Murchison Falls on the Nile River in western Uganda.

My spirits rose as we drove out of Nairobi. In spite of the discomforts and sometimes primitive accommodations, I never got tired of going on safari, leaving behind the cocktail parties, the dinners, the visiting VIPs, and escaping into the wide emptiness of African sky and bush, into the Kenya I had come to love best.

Our safari began like a long roller coaster ride, from Nairobi up to Limuru, then down the escarpment to the floor of the Rift Valley, past Naivasha to Nakuru. At Lake Nakuru thousands of flamingoes took flight as we passed, turning the sky pink. After climbing the escarpment on the far side of the Rift, the road leveled off as it headed west toward Kampala, capitol of Uganda. The countryside turned jungle green and lush, the air soggy. Perspiration soaked our hair and clothes. In the small villages we passed through, groves of orange and lemon trees, coconut palms, and leafy banana trees crowded around rectangular mud-and-wattle houses set on patches of scraped red earth.

At Jinja a power plant marked the source of the Nile where it rises out of Lake Victoria. British explorers Burton, Speke, and Baker had come this way, cutting through jungle and bush in their search for the birthplace of the great river. I strained to see the Nile rushing out of the Lake there, at Ripon Falls, and was disappointed to see no falls, only the power plant and a dam, with water sliding sedately over it, controlled and regulated by the hand of man. Ripon Falls is no more.

Kampala, like Rome, is a city built on hills. On the crest of one, as we approached the city, the onion domes of a graceful white mosque caught the sunlight. In the city itself, broad avenues led past shops, office buildings, and the campus of Makerere College to the fine big hotel where we stayed. After tea, while the children played in the park across the street I sat, limp, on a bench, too hot to move. During the night, ceiling fans turned slow paddles over our heads, stirring up tiny waves of stifling air.

Uganda for centuries had had a cruel and bloody history under the rule of the country's largest tribe, the Baganda, headed by the Kabaka. In the 1950's, as a British Protectorate and still nominally ruled by the current Kabaka, it was enjoying a period of relative peace. There were rumors of tribal tensions and rivalries, of corruption at high levels, but to visitors like us, Kampala was a beautiful city dreaming amidst flowers in the damp tropical heat. We left two days later oblivious of the dark future that lay ahead. Under Idi Amin the wide tree-lined streets would soon lie in rubble, filled with khaki-clad soldiers and bands of rebels fighting and marauding through the city. Countless thousands of Africans would die during the years of fighting. Europeans would leave when the violence reached crisis proportions, or lock themselves in their homes until a brief calm returned. It would be many years before peace was restored to Uganda.

But that morning we drove out of Kampala without a backward glance. A tantalizing aroma rose from the brown paper sackful of Indian *samosas* on the seat beside me. We quenched their fire with a squeeze of fresh lime juice and washed them down with cold beer and orange squash—what else?—for the children.

Several hours later, inside the protection of Murchison Falls National Park, elephants dominated the rolling grasslands. They browsed in family groups, stood in pools of water spraying themselves with their trunks, meandered in long files beside the road. Several times we stopped to let them cross. Ambling along, they paid no attention to us, though we could almost have reached out and touched the gray, wrinkled skin. Sadly, the elephants were gone from the Park for many years, victims of political chaos and merciless poaching under Idi Amin. Their numbers are only now slowly recovering.

The safari lodge, run by the Uganda government, perched high on a bluff overlooking the Nile. To the west rose the misty outlines of the Ruwenzori—the Mountains of the Moon—and beyond them lay the Congo. The Nile, shining blue, wound peacefully north through green hills on its long journey to Egypt. I couldn't in my wildest dreams have imagined the violent destiny that awaited not only Uganda but, only a year later, those deceptively tranquil lands across the river in the Belgian Congo.

Our accommodations were primitive. Far beyond the reach of electricity or indoor plumbing, we relied on safari lamps and outhouses. The food we were

served in the dining room was prepared on a kerosene stove. The kerosene flavored everything we ate, even the puddings. When we went out game watching,
the staff provided us with lunches that included a thermos of an unidentifiable
but familiar brown beverage that we had had before, in other East African hotel
thermoses. We called it "coftea." This time a hint of kerosene had been added.

Just upstream from the Lodge were the Falls, where a narrow cleft in the rock
cliffs squeezes the Nile like a giant hand until, boiling and frothing with pent-up
energy, the river escapes and crashes down the cliff face. Clouds of spray hang like
smoke over the rocks and the river. Far below, the green water is churned into
eddies and whirlpools until gradually it widens and smoothes between grassy
banks.

We boarded a small river launch for the trip up to the Falls. Our family of five,
plus the boatman, filled it to capacity. As we putt-putted up the river—had we
boarded the African Queen, I wondered?—hippos as big as the boat bumped
against the hull. Looking back, it seems like a recipe for disaster, but like the time
with the lions at Amboseli, I was too spellbound to remember to worry. Somno-
lent giants, the hippos spend their days drowsing in the water and feeding lazily
on plants on the river bottom. At night they lumber out to devour the grass on
the banks. Lying on our cots in the Lodge, we could hear them snorting and
snuffling from dark to dawn.

From the boat, we saw crocodiles dozing on the banks, jaws agape. The children amused themselves by throwing Smarties, the British version of M&M's,
into the toothy mouths and watching the giant jaws snap shut. Elephants browsing beside the river were almost hidden by the stands of tall elephant grass.

We were awed by the power of the Falls, viewed from our small boat beneath
them as close as it was safe to go. Wet spray drenched us and currents of cool air
fanned our faces. Later we drove up a dirt road to the top of the Falls and looked
down on them from above. They thundered into the abyss, leaping under that
tremendous pressure over the edge of the cliff. Bob climbed down the rocks
alongside the Falls with Cathy and Robbie to take some pictures.

Walking back to the car with Kelly, I lost my way in the elephant grass. It was
tall—way over my head—and blotted out the whole world. We might have been
the last two people on earth. We had seen no boats on the river, no other cars on
the road to the Falls. The voices of Bob and the two older children had long since
been drowned out by the crashing water.

My stomach knotted and my heart began to pound. An elephant could blun-
der out of the jungle of grass at any moment. And here was Kelly, her hand nestled trustingly in mine, piping up, "Isn't this fun, Mommy?" as we pushed our

way through the grass forest. Pollen filled our eyes and nostrils and powdered Kelly's jeans and small blue sneakers.

Holding her hand tightly, I walked steadily away from the sound of the Falls. After what seemed an interminable length of time, we found our way out of the elephant grass and back to the safety of the car. We met no elephants.

As our car turned back toward the Lodge, rays of the descending sun slanted under dark clouds that hung from the dome of the sky. The bright neon light turned the vegetation a lurid green and the river to gray silver. Kelly and I had escaped unharmed. I relaxed and lost myself in the starkly beautiful landscape before me.

Robbie, Kelly, and Cathy in the boat on the Nile

Hippos in the Nile River

Crocodile along the Nile.

Elephant beside the Nile

Murchison Falls on the Nile

22

KWA HERI MEANS GOODBYE

Too soon it was November again. Our two-year tour of duty was over, and it was time to go home. Our orders had come: we were to leave Kenya right after Thanksgiving and would be home for Christmas. The children were ecstatic about going home to grandparents, friends, their old school, hamburgers, pizza, milk shakes, and American TV. But once their joy at being back in the United States faded a little, nostalgia for East Africa would emerge. They would miss the friends of so many different backgrounds, the safaris we had taken through a wild landscape where exotic animals ran free, the excitement of a life very different from anything they had known before. They would even miss some of the food, like marmite and *samosas* and curried fried peas.

Bob and I were torn. We had come to love Kenya and its friendly people, its green forested highlands, its endless brown plains that changed color with every shifting cloud and angle of the sun. I loved being out there under the enormous African sky, loved the quality of light, the feeling of freedom and soaring exhilaration when I looked across mile after empty mile, with nothing between me and the edge of the world except a thorn tree or a giraffe's tall profile on the far horizon.

American author Tony Hiss, who writes about the influence of "place" on the human psyche, believes that the loss of great tracts of our American prairies, so much like the African savannas, has changed us in subtle ways. With the conversion of open land into cities and farms, we have lost the experience of aloneness in the vastness of nature, the sense of a greater universe that puts human concerns in their proper perspective and calms our souls. Perhaps, deep inside me, unconscious yearning for that lost experience had been satisfied on the grasslands of Africa.

Cathy holds a friend's pet monkey.

Robbie dares to hold the monkey.

It would be hard to leave. Sitting on a carton of books in the front hall of our house, I looked around at empty rooms. The packers had finished; the movers would come the next day. Our last few days would be spent at the Norfolk. We had come full circle.

For the moment, I was alone. The children were spending the day with friends; Bob was at his office clearing out a few last papers. Mukolwe and Rachel had already left for new jobs, and Marikus was in the hospital with a bleeding ulcer. Only Ali was still out back in the quarters, keeping watch over the house for one more day.

Rachel and I had clasped our hands in a lingering handshake, smiling into each other's eyes. "*Kwa heri*, Rachel," I said. "*Asante kabisa!*" Thank you totally, altogether, completely. Probably ungrammatical, but the best I could muster in Swahili. I yearned to put my arms around her and hug this woman who had taken such devoted care of Kelly, who had watched over her on their many walks, had taught her to speak Swahili, had sat with her in the garden for countless hours while she played. But Africans seldom showed affection in public. Once again, I hesitated to intrude in some unsuspected realm of cultural taboos. Our handshake would have to do.

Marikus and I bade each other a different farewell. His troubles were never ending. Most of the time he brought them on himself, but sometimes he just seemed destined for disaster. I had been stunned when a major *shauri* (argument) erupted involving Rachel's daughter, Filois. She had graduated from the Ludwigs' mission school and had come to Nairobi to live temporarily with her mother. One morning I had heard angry shouts in the back yard and a most unusual flood of furious Swahili from Rachel, followed by an hysterical weeping and wailing in Marikus's unmistakable jarring tones. By the time I reached the kitchen door, Marikus was carrying on like a madman. The usually calm Rachel, exploding like a wrathful African volcano, had accused Marikus of propositioning Filois. From the fierce expression on her face, I expected her any minute to pick him up bodily and heave him across the yard.

When he saw me in the doorway, Marikus burst out at top volume with denials.

"*Hapana*, memsahib, is not true. These people are all against me. They are all telling lies, memsahib!"

Filois stood beside her mother, staring at the ground. Rachel continued to glare furiously at Marikus. Ali, hovering near Rachel and Filois, looked distressed.

Bit by bit I pried the story from Filois. She said that whenever she was alone in the quarters, Marikus would offer her money to sleep with him. Though she repeatedly said no, he continued to pester her, so that morning she had finally told her mother. Rachel was, predictably, livid.

I was convinced Filois was telling the truth, and I too was angry at Marikus. I sent him into the kitchen to begin preparations for the dinner party we were giving that night, and suggested to Rachel that after that Filois should come into our house with her mother instead of remaining alone in the quarters. That seemed to satisfy them both. Rachel's face resumed its usual placid expression. Filois ventured a shy smile.

I found Marikus working at the sink in sullen silence, angrily washing vegetables. Ali looked up as I entered the kitchen, then looked away quickly.

"Marikus!" I said. "There will be no more shauris with Filois! You, and your "brothers" too (he seemed to have dozens, whether real or tribal) stay away from her, or your job is *kwisha*, finished, and Bwana and I will not help you find another when we leave. *Unasikia*? You understand?"

"Yes, memsahib," he muttered, scrubbing potatoes furiously. We continued to work, mostly in silence, for the rest of the morning.

Marikus apparently took my threat to heart, because there were no more shauris involving Filois. But almost immediately we had a more serious crisis. News came from Kisumu that Joyce and baby Edward were very ill with a fever. "But haven't Joyce and the baby gone to the hospital, or seen a doctor?" I asked.

"No, memsahib," Marikus answered sadly. "No hospital is near our village, and clinic is very far."

Bob had wired Joyce money for bus fare and two days later she and the baby arrived. The Nairobi doctor diagnosed malaria and began treating them both. One night Marikus awakened me with a frantic pounding on my bedroom window. Joyce was hemorrhaging and he didn't know what to do.

Bob was away, and I couldn't leave the children alone in the house, so I called an ambulance and Joyce was taken to the hospital. The doctors stopped the bleeding and next day she came home. Marikus said the doctors told him she was pregnant again. When both she and the baby recovered, Joyce took Edward back to their village, but Marikus continued to worry. He also began complaining about his stomach, and then one morning he came to me and said he had had "much blood" in the night. "She came from here," he said, pointing behind him with a graphic gesture. I took him to Dr. Mwathi, who diagnosed a bleeding ulcer and put him in the hospital. I visited him daily, half-holding my breath each time I made my way down the long, rank-smelling ward, taking milk and puddings to supplement the poor hospital food, and stationery and stamps so Marikus could write to Joyce through the village interpreter. He was recovering rapidly and was relieved when I told him I had found him a job with another American family. He was to go to them as soon as he left the hospital. The last time I saw him, he was sitting up in his cot, grinning cheerfully as he said kwa heri.

We were back home in the States by the time Marikus wrote that the new baby, whom he called "the follower of Edward," was born prematurely and had died. I was shocked, but Marikus, though I'm sure he grieved, was more philosophical than I.

"Joyce will have many more children, memsahib," he wrote. "Soon another baby will come."

I would be left with a haunting question. Had I allowed Joyce and Edward to stay permanently in Marikus's crowded little room, with a hospital and doctors nearby, might Edward's baby brother have been born healthy, and might he still be alive? Once again I had been caught up in a system that I had no power to change.

Ali came into the front hall, putting an end to my musings. At my urging he sat down on a nearby carton, for the first time ever in my presence, and offered me one of his strong East African cigarettes. For a while we sat smoking in companionable silence. Then, "I'll miss you, Ali," I said. Miss your cheery laugh, your bright smile, your energy and enthusiasm and eagerness to help.

"'Miss,' memsahib?" he asked, puzzled. I didn't know any Swahili word for 'miss.' I groped for a way to explain.

"When I get home to America I'll think of you and Rachel, and wish to be here," I said.

"Someday you come back," he replied. He stood up, his face somber. "*Kwa heri*, memsahib," he said, and bowed as he always did when he said goodnight.

"*Kwa heri*, Ali." I clasped his hand for a long moment, then blinked back tears as he walked down the hall and back out to his quarters. I was not saying farewell just to Ali. His leaving symbolized the end of our life in this house and of our two years in Kenya.

I sat for a while longer in the empty hall. I had come to Kenya knowing little about the country or its people, and had quickly relinquished my preconceptions about naked savages in steaming jungles. On the adventures our family had shared I had discovered, buried deep in my security-loving soul, a willingness to respond to the challenge of the unknown. These adventures, these new experiences, had brought our family closer. The shared memories formed the basis of a rich store of family stories that would forge strong bonds among us in the future.

Years later our grandson, another Robbie, who has never been to Africa, would say, "Whenever our family gets together, you all end up talking about Africa!"

Bob and I too had grown closer. In Washington, his work had been remote, his professional life an isolated existence, an hour's commute from our suburban home. I had rarely been in his office and knew most of his colleagues only by name. In Kenya, by contrast, I was much more a partner, a member of the official American family with some shared responsibilities for official entertaining and for promoting good relations with people in Kenya. Often, on the way home from a dinner or reception, we would "talk shop" about the people we had met or spoken to that evening, what we had heard about the political situation in Kenya, how the talks about independence were going in London. It made me feel much more a part of that other half of Bob's life.

The personal friends I had made during these two years had enriched and enlivened my life: Jemima Gecaga, who combined successfully the roles of career woman, wife, and mother, when to do so was rare; Rani Khurana, with whom I gardened, cooked, laughed, drank tea, and talked about India, Singapore, America, and our children; Ruth Njiiri, who helped me imagine how it felt to be black; Chief Njiiri and the Njoroges and all the other Africans and Asians who had welcomed us so warmly into their country and into their lives. I would go home with an altered and broadened view of this part of the world, and with a sense of identification with the women of Asia and East Africa.

I was also going home with this newly discovered confidence. Many of the experiences I had had here, but especially the safari to Malindi, had nurtured in me a new spirit of independence, a determination to value my roles of wife, mother, homemaker as much as ever, but to reach beyond them. I had made up my mind that I would register for graduate school, resume my teaching career...Who could say where it would all lead? Anticipation of the future coursed through me, even while regret over leaving Kenya was pulling me back.

On our next-to-last night in Kenya our African friends held a party at the Gecagas.' More than forty people came, including Tom Mboya, who had driven for six hours from a speech-making tour upcountry in order to be with us. Mareka and Jemima had roasted a goat, and there were speeches and gifts: Kikuyu earrings for me, and for Bob a monkey fur rug, an elder's hat, and a fly whisk, symbol of wisdom and authority. As a final tribute Bob was made an honorary member of the Kikuyu tribe.

We left Nairobi at night. A crowd of friends—African, Asian, American, and British—had gathered at the airport to say good-bye. I looked into the many familiar faces and felt as though I were leaving a part of me behind, as though I might never be quite whole again.

The plane tipped its wings toward the lights of Nairobi as it circled one last time, then pointed north toward Ethiopia. I stared down into darkness as complete as when we had flown to Nairobi two years before. Kenya lay there below me, invisible but no longer a mystery, no longer unknown.

"*Kwa heri*," I whispered. Then, "Someday I'll be back!" I wanted to shout into the black void. It was a promise I would keep.

Cathy, Rachel, and Kelly at the Norfolk Hotel. Rachel comes to say a second goodbye.

Our family and Chumley with an American visitor

EPILOGUE

In the two years we lived there, Kenya moved closer to independence than any of us would have believed possible. As we prepared to leave, conferences were being held in London to discuss steps toward African self-government. The speed with which political changes took place was due partly to the Colonial Office, under pressure from Prime Minister Macmillan and the British Labour Party, partly to the negotiations of a few liberal white and Asian members of the Kenya Government, and partly to the leadership of men like Tom Mboya and Gikonyo Kiano.

A second general election in which Africans could vote had been held in 1958, and Gikonyo had been elected to a seat in Legislative Council, joining Tom. Africans no longer had to carry the hated passbooks, or be checked through police blocks when they moved in and out of Nairobi or the reserves.

In a new African housing development built by the government, the Njiiris and Kianos were living in small private bungalows with cement floors and indoor plumbing—far from luxurious but vastly superior to anything previously available to them or other Africans. The Kianos, at the Nairobi business school they had opened, were turning out young African secretaries and clerks. Kariuki Njiiri was promoting literacy among the villagers, a few Maasai children were beginning to come in from the manyatas to go to school, and my girls at the Y would soon be ready to go out into the world and start their careers. Hundreds of African students were attending American colleges and universities, learning skills they would need to govern an independent Kenya. And shortly before we left, Bob had lunch at the New Stanley Hotel with Gikonyo and Tom. There were shocked, disbelieving stares from the other diners, but no angry protests. And they were served.

There were still obstacles, of course, in the way of Africans trying to establish themselves in this changing Kenya, especially in the professions. Mungai Njoroge had returned to Kenya a few months before, and for a while had practiced medicine in the Kikuyu Reserve. He confided to us that it was difficult and frustrating to adapt his training in clean, well-equipped American hospitals to the unhygienic conditions in the villages. Furthermore, his attempts to set up a modest clinic in Thika met with resistance. With strict segregation still firmly in place,

European and Asian landlords (few if any were African) did not trust this rare phenomenon, an American-educated African doctor, and were unwilling to risk renting him space. With Bob to vouch for him, Mungai finally persuaded an Asian landlord to lease him a storefront, where he opened his clinic. When Independence came in 1963, he gave up his practice to become personal physician to President Jomo Kenyatta, as well as Minister of Health and later, Minister of Defense.

We were leaving a Kenya already plunging forward into the future. It would remain for many years one of the most stable and prosperous countries in Africa.

Jomo Kenyatta in beaded hat. Dr. Gikonyo Kiano on steps, wearing glasses

GLOSSARY

Amerikani—unbleached calico cloth
asante sana—thank you very much
askari—soldier, guard, policeman
ayah—nanny
bado kidogo—soon, not yet, in a little while
banda—a large shed, usually without walls
bwana—master, mister, sir
chai—tea
choo—toilet
dactari—doctor
dawa—medicine
dudu, wadudu—insect, insects
duka—shop
fundi—skilled workman
hapa—here
hapana—no
hii—this
jambo—hello
kahawa—coffee
kali—sharp in temper, cross, fierce (also sharp, as a knife)
kanga—a piece of cloth worn by women
kanzu—a long-sleeved ankle-length outer garment worn by men
kikapu—a flexible woven basket with two small handles
kufa—to die
kuja—to come
kusikia—to understand, hear
kwa heri—goodbye
kwenda—to go
kwisha—to finish, come to an end
leo—today
makaa (plural)—charcoal
manyata—Maasai homestead

mbaya—bad
memsahib—mistress, lady
mingi—much, many
moja—one
mtoto—child
mzee—an old person
mzuri—good, nice
ndio—yes
ngoma—dance, drum
nne—four
panga—machete or large knife
posho—daily supply of food, commonly referring to corn meal
rafiki—friend
safari—trip, journey
samosas—Indian food item consisting of triangles of crispy fried dough filled with meat and/or vegetables
sana—very
shamba—garden, farm
shauri—discussion, debate, often heated
sucari—sugar
tafadhali—please
thingira—men's house, lodge (Kikuyu)
uhuru—freedom
yako—your, yours
yangu—my, mine

978-0-595-41517-5
0-595-41517-2

CPSIA information can be obtained at www.ICGtesting.com
Printed in the USA
BVOW05s1630250814

364162BV00001B/63/P